A HISTORY OF CYCLING IN 100 OBJECTS

SUZE CLEMITSON

BLOOMSBURY

LONDON · OXFORD · NEW YORK · NEW DELHI · SYDNEY

Bloomsbury Sport
An imprint of Bloomsbury Publishing Plc

50 Bedford Square
London
WC1B 3DP
UK

1385 Broadway
New York
NY 10018
USA

www.bloomsbury.com

BLOOMSBURY and the Diana logo are trademarks of
Bloomsbury Publishing Plc

First published in 2017
Text © Suze Clemitson, 2017
Cover illustrations by Simon Scarsbrook

British Library Cataloguing-in-Publication Data
A catalogue record for this book is available from the British
Library.

ISBN: Print: 978-1-4729-1888-8
         ePDF: 978-1-4729-1890-1
         ePub: 978-1-4729-1889-5

1 2 3 4 5 6 7 8 9 10

Typeset in Archer
Designed by Nimbus Design
Printed and bound in China by RR Donnelley Asia
Printing Solutions Limited

Bloomsbury Publishing Plc makes every effort to ensure that
the papers used in the manufacture of our books are natural,
recyclable products made from wood grown in well-managed
forests. Our manufacturing processes conform to the
environmental regulations of the country of origin.

To find out more about our authors and books visit
www.bloomsbury.com. Here you will find extracts, author
interviews, details of forthcoming events and the option to sign
up for our newsletters.

Photo Acknowledgements

Pages 7, 9, 11, 13, 15, 17, 21, 27, 31, 33, 35, 37, 39, 43, 47, 51,
57, 59, 61, 63, 71, 73, 79, 87, 89, 93, 97, 99, 101, 105, 107,
109, 111, 115, 117, 119, 121, 123, 125, 131, 137, 139, 145, 147,
149, 151, 153, 159, 167, 175, 177, 179, 183, 185, 189, 195,
203, 205, 213, 215, 217, 219, 221 © Getty Images

Pages 23, 25, 65, 67, 75, 81, 157, 161, 163, 165, 169, 171, 173,
181, 187, 193, 197, 201, 207, 209, 211 © L'Equipe/Offside

Page 19 © the Marin Museum of Bicycling

Page 41 © M&N/Alamy Stock Photo

Page 45 © Sturmey-Archer Heritage

Page 49 © Gerard Brown

Pages 53 and 55 provided by Google Patents

Page 69 © Castelli

Page 83 © H. A. Roth, provided by ASSOS S.A.

Page 91 © Carson Blume

Page 85 © Arne Mill/frontalvision

Page 113 courtesy of the Wellcome Collection

Page 127 © Bloomsbury Publishing

Page 129 © David Taylor

Page 133 © Edd Westmacott/Alamy Stock Photo

Page 135 © Dave Walker

Page 141 courtesy of the University of California
Libraries

Page 142 © Schwinn, courtesy of Pacific-Cycle

Contents

AUTHOR'S ACKNOWLEDGEMENTS

My thanks, as ever, to Charlotte Croft and Sarah Connelly at Bloomsbury for their unfailing support and skill at doing what they do so effortlessly well.

To Lucy Doncaster for her editorial flair and being so easy to work with and Nik Cook for casting a constructively critical and expertly technical eye across these pages.

Thanks also to the Co-The Cafe in Brantome for keeping me supplied with fabulous coffee and endless free WiFi when I had neither.

To every cycling writer who has written lucidly, coherently and brilliantly about the technical innovations that created cycling as both a sport and a pastime, my undying thanks for making my research so pleasurable.

And as ever, to my brilliant family, without whom I would never have written a word.

The Bicycles

1 Draisine

It starts, quite literally, with a big bang. When Mount Tambora in Indonesia erupted in 1815, massive quantities of carbon dioxide entered the atmosphere and caused temperatures to drop worldwide, including Europe. In the 'Year Without A Summer' that followed, crops across the region failed and famine and disease set in, resulting in horses being slaughtered for food and to save money and resources. Society now needed an alternative to costly horsepower, which is where Baron Karl von Drais' big democratic idea of a (human) muscle-powered machine comes in.

Known variously around Europe as the Laufmaschine (the German for 'running machine'); Draisine (after its inventor, Karl Friedrich Christian Ludwig, Baron Drais von Sauerbronn); vélocipède (the French for 'fast feet'); and 'hobby horse' or 'dandy horse' in England (on account of the fact that it was deemed an expensive toy for rich dandies), the Draisine was a simple affair. Consisting of little more than a plank of wood joining two equal-sized wheels with a rudimentary saddle and steering system attached, it was used initially by Drais – who was at that time working as a forester for the Grand Duke of Baden – as a fast means of getting around his employer's estate. Realising its potential, the intrepid Baron jumped astride his invention on 12 June, 1817 in the centre of Mannheim, he travelled 16km (10 miles) in just over an hour, marking the inception of horseless transport.

The Draisine was based on a simple premise that enabled riders to sit astride a frame and run along – much like children's balance bikes of today. A good idea in principle; in practice the terrible state of European roads made striding and balancing both dangerous and uncomfortable and the design was soon superseded.

In England, in 1818, just a year after the Draisine's inaugural outing, London-based coach-maker Denis Johnson began manufacturing his 'hobby horse', which was a lighter, improved version of the Draisine featuring larger wheels and, for the ladies, a model with a dropped, curved frame that was easier to mount in style. This proved very popular among the wealthy classes and the craze soon reached the USA, where many examples were made and could be hired for use in one of the specially constructed riding rinks (similar to skating rinks, but made of wood). Despite its popularity, however, the fad was short-lived because its lack of practical use along with its nickname, the 'dandy horse'. By the 1820s, the Draisine and its imitators were a footnote in transport history.

But what of the man behind the machine? Born into a noble family in 1785, in Karlsruhe, Germany, Drais was a democrat whose egalitarian views got him into trouble with both his aristocratic peers and the authorities. A supporter of the failed German Revolution of 1848, he had previously spent several years in exile in Brazil, survived an assassination attempt in 1838, and been very much a persona non grata in high society. Despite these factors, this one-time civil servant and professor of mechanics was prolific in his inventions, which included a meat grinder that is still used today, a typewriter, a machine to record piano music on paper, a stenotype machine and a quadricycle. It was the Draisine, however, for which he is most remembered because it set in motion a series of inventions that would eventually culminate in the modern bicycle. Drais never saw a penny – as a civil servant he wasn't allowed to patent his invention – and the government pension he received was stripped away by the Royalists in the aftermath of the revolution. He died penniless in Karlsruhe in 1851.

The hobby horse, invented in 1817, was the big bang for the modern bicycle. Hobby horses had no pedals or brakes, instead they were propelled by the rider pushing on the ground with his feet and dragging to slow the machine.

② Boneshaker or vélocipède

If the Draisine was the Big Bang for the bicycle, then the missing link between hobby horses and pedal power was the boneshaker or vélocipède (the latter name had also been used for the Draisine, but became a generic term for a human-powered wheeled land vehicle with the advent of the boneshaker in the 1860s).

This missing link was heavy and horribly uncomfortable to ride, often leaving its passengers black and blue after a spin (which accounts for its English nickname). Despite this, the boneshaker was important because it enabled riders to travel far greater distances than the Draisine, and with their feet off the ground, all because it possessed a rudimentary set of pedals.

Two men vie to take credit for the vélocipède, both of them French. Between them they created the basic mechanism that, after a 40-year lull when bicycles fell from popular regard, transformed the Draisine or hobby horse from a rich man's toy into a true bicycle. First came carriage-maker Pierre Lallement. By adding a rotary crank to the Draisine's front wheel in the early 1860s, he realised that a rider could go considerably further than was possible using running power. Recognising its potential and in need of cash, in 1863 or 1864 Lallement sold the design to the Olivier brothers, who formed a partnership with blacksmith Pierre Michaux in 1868 and produced the popular Michauline.

In 1865, Lallement emigrated to the USA, where on 4 April, 1866 he demonstrated his invention by riding from Ansonia, New York to New Haven, Connecticut – a distance of nearly 80km (50 miles) – the first long-distance ride on American soil. Later that month he filed the first-ever patent for a pedal-powered bike. Sadly, unable to attract investors and suspected of stealing the idea from his former employer in France, the young immigrant was discredited and the patents ended up in the hands of the Columbia bicycle company, which made a fortune from manufacturing them at the end of the 19th century. Lallement himself died penniless in Boston in 1891, aged 47, his role in the development of the bicycle until recently largely forgotten.

But it is Pierre Michaux whom the history books generally honour as the creator of the first modern bicycle. However, this is where the plot thickens. Michaux is said to have added cranks and pedals to the front wheel of a Draisine in the 1860s while working in partnership with his son Ernest and… you guessed it, Pierre Lallement. Did Lallement steal Michaux's idea and rush to America to patent it? Or did Michaux simply copy an idea his business partner had developed? One thing is certain: Michaux gained French patent #80637 in 1868 for 'an improvement in the construction of bicycles', two years after Lallement had patented his very similar idea.

Whoever actually came up with the design, it was Michaux who mass-produced the vélocipède, adapting the originally all-wood construction and making it from cast iron, for ease of manufacture. Incredibly heavy and somewhat prone to breaking, these cast-iron frames were later superseded by wrought-iron ones, meaning they were stronger and lighter, but still incredibly uncomfortable to ride. This, coupled with the fact that competing manufacturers were making stronger bikes to a modified design, resulted in both the demise of the Michauline specifically and the fall from favour of bicycling in general in France and the USA around 1870.

But by this time the bicycle bug had spread far beyond mainland Europe and America, especially among the youth of the British Isles, which was now to become the hub of the next phase in the bicycle's evolution.

With its rudimentary pedals, the boneshaker was the missing link in cycling's evolution. The innovative addition of cranks and pedals attached to the front wheel improved on the earlier hobby horse, which was powered by the rider pushing along the ground with their feet.

3 'Ordinary' or penny-farthing

Known variously during their heyday as the 'high-wheeler', 'hi-wheel', 'ordinary' or, most commonly, as 'bicycle', these iconic vélocipèdes bridged the design gap between the boneshaker of the 1860s and early 1870s and the safety bicycles that emerged in the late 1890s. The nickname 'penny-farthing' came later, from the fact that when viewed side-on the huge front wheel and tiny back wheel resembled two old English coins.

Before the introduction of a gearing mechanism, the only way to increase the distance travelled per revolution of the front wheel was to make it bigger. But how could you create a wheel that maintained its structure while being light enough to be turned by a simple pedal stroke? Enter Frenchman Eugène Meyer, who in 1868 produced an all-metal wheel that relied on lighter tensioned wire spokes rather than traditional wooden ones, an advance that paved the way for the evolution of the 'ordinary'.

All it needed was a genius to pull together the various design elements that made up this icon of Victorian engineering. This was James Starley, rightly considered the father of the modern bike industry. Entirely self-taught, his curiosity and inventiveness was limitless, and he was the living embodiment of the entrepreneurial spirit of the age.

Born in Sussex in 1831, Starley started his working life on a farm, demonstrating his budding talent for invention by creating rat traps. In his early teens, the young inventor went to London to work as an gardener, using his spare time to repair watches and other machinery. Aware of his talents, Starley's employer, John Penn, asked him to fix an expensive sewing machine that had broken down. After repairing the machine, Starley went on to make improvements to it, impressing his master, who luckily knew Josiah Turner, a partner of the company that had made the machine: Newton, Wilson and Company.

In 1859, Starley started working in their London-based factory, before joining forces with Turner and forming the Coventry Sewing Machine Company in 1861. In 1868, Starley was introduced to a French boneshaker by Turner's nephew. The rest is history. The company switched from making sewing machines to manufacturing bicycles, soon becoming the epicentre of the British bicycle industry.

Starley's all-metal high-wheelers were works of art, costing more than the average worker's annual wage. The most popular was the Ariel, after the spirit in Shakespeare's *The Tempest*. Advertised as 'the lightest, strongest, and most elegant of modern bicycles', it soon became popular among well-off young men. The high-wheeler had two great advantages over the boneshaker: its enormous front wheel handled ruts and potholes with ease, and it had a top speed of 40kph, to encourage a craze for 'ordinary' racing, which attracted huge crowds throughout the 1870s and 1880s.

With wheels 2m in diameter – and sometimes more – riding an 'ordinary' required both athletic prowess and determination. With the rider perched vertiginously on top of the front wheel, the 'ordinary' looked anything but. It was dangerous, too – riders casually described hitting the deck face first from a height of 3m (10ft) or so as 'taking a header' or 'coming a cropper' – and was responsible for a rash of serious neck injuries. One history of the period claimed that a collision with a pedestrian at 19kph would result in certain death for both parties and that 3000 fatalities a year could be laid at the door of this unstable and perilous machine.

There had to be a better way to bring the cycling revolution to the masses. And James Starley was about to come up with just the thing...

The penny-farthing bridged the gap between the boneshaker and the safety bicycle. Here, a penny-farthing race on the Herne Hill bicycle race track in London in 1932.

4 Tricycle

In a world of whizzy balance bikes, the tricycle is now regarded as a slightly old-fashioned children's toy. However, during the bicycle craze that gripped the world in the 1890s it once threatened to topple the two-wheeler and become the bicycle of choice.

The tricycle was around in some form or another long before the Draisine appeared on the scene. But the word 'tricycle', literally meaning 'three-wheeled', was first used in France in the 1820s to describe any tri-wheeled, lever-driven conveyance. However, these were little more than adapted carriages, and were unpopular with a wider audience. Cue James Starley and his nephew John Kemp Starley, whose vision made the three-wheeler an attractive and functional proposition with their series-produced hand-operated, lever-driven Coventry of 1876 (later renamed the Coventry Lever Tricycle). The Starleys were obsessed with perfecting the design of a machine that could be mounted safely at ground level. In 1877 John Kemp Starley went into business with local cycling enthusiast William Sutton, to form Starley and Sutton Co. This company developed and manufactured tricycles, and a few years later these were branded as Rover.

With its wide wheelbase capable of accommodating a two-person seat, or one lady clad in crinoline, the tricycle was a hit with women, who were becoming interested in the idea of riding for fitness, pleasure and the independence cycling gave them. One such intrepid female tricyclist was Miss Roach of the Isle of Wight, the daughter of the local Starley agent. Her speed, grace and skill so impressed Queen Victoria as she flashed past her horse carriage, and when she demonstrated the device to the Queen at Osborne House, that the Royal lady went on to order not one but two of the same model, the Salvo Quad, in 1881, earning it the nickname the 'Royal Salvo'.

By the 1890s, more than 120 different models were being produced by 20 British manufacturers. Tricycles were being exported to the Antipodes, to India and all across Europe, and even made in-roads into the American market. Everyone from Maharajas to British Prime Minister Lord Salisbury rode them, the latter choosing to tricycle around his estate as a hobby, accompanied by a footman to push him up any hills.

When it was first launched, few expected the tricycle to challenge the popularity of the bicycle. They were wrong. Solid, stable, easy to stop and start, and able to accommodate some luggage as well as a second rider, the tricycle was an ideal tourer – and manufacturers were keen to promote it as such. In 1882, when a Mr A. Bird rode 222 miles on a Humber tricycle from Cambridge and back in 24 hours – only 20 miles short of the two-wheel distance record – cycling manufacturers wondered if the future might lie with three wheels, not two.

In the end it was John Kemp Starley's Rover of 1884 that proved the undoing of the tricycle, the very machine he had helped to popularise. This revolutionary new bike borrowed from the technology of the tricycle, utilising their chain drives to produce a machine with two equal-sized wheels that allowed its rider to place both feet safely on the floor when not in motion. Both male and female tricyclists soon adopted the new 'safety bicycle' and all other models faded into the pale.

Despite this massive shift towards safety bicycles, though, tricycle production continued into the 20th century, and many graceful models influenced by art deco were produced. By the 1960s the tricycle had been relegated to being a children's toy, now manufactured in plastic with brightly coloured frames. However, a niche but active trike racing scene still exists in the UK.

An illustration featuring different types of tricycles and bicycles. The tricycle challenged the two-wheeler for supremacy in the 1890s. Top row: the Otto Bicycle and the Rover Safety. Middle row: the Apollo Tricycle and the King of Clubs. Bottom row: the Humber Tricycle and the Singer's Straight Steerer.

TRICYCLE.

AND OTHER FORMS OF CYCLES.

PLATE 2.

7. The "Otto" Bicycle.

8. The "Rover" Safety.

9. The "Apollo" Tricycle.

10. The "King of Clubs."

11. The "Humber" Tricycle.

12. The Singer's "Straight Steerer."

⑤ Rover Safety Bicycle

If James Starley created the British bicycle industry, then his nephew, John Kemp Starley, made bikes available to everyone. Starley's aim was simple, to: 'place the rider at the proper distance from the ground', so that they could: 'exert the greatest force upon the pedals with the least amount of fatigue.' The first Rover Safety Bicycle was built in 1884 at Starley and Sutton Co's factory, Meteor Works, in Coventry and went on to revolutionise transport and cycling history.

But why was this particular bicycle so important? If you compare a photo of the Rover Safety of 1885 with a modern bicycle, the similarities are immediate: a diamond-shaped frame; two even wheels; a chain drive connecting frame-mounted pedals and cranks to the rear wheel. This is the great granddaddy of them all – a simple yet revolutionary design that finally made the Starleys' dream a reality. According to the magazine *Cyclist* (now *Cycling Weekly*), it 'set the fashion for the world.'

The Rover Safety Bicycle, so-called to differentiate it from the dangerous 'ordinary', wasn't a new idea, more the amalgamation of several design developments in one improved package. Innovators included André Guilmet, a French watchmaker, who used his expertise to develop a frame-mounted hub connected to the rear wheels by means of a chain-driven mechanism in the late 1860s; Thomas Wiseman and Frederick Shearing, who published their designs for a 'safety bike' in *The English Mechanic* in 1869; and Harry Lawson, who produced his Bicyclette Safety Bike in 1879. However, it was the Rover that pulled these ideas, and those of J.K. Starley's uncle, James, into a coherent design that is the blueprint of all modern bikes.

The early Rovers of 1884, equipped with a 91.5cm (36in) front wheel and a 76cm (30in) back wheel and bridle rods rather than a raked front fork, were far from perfect, but the company worked hard to modify the design and launched the Rover II in 1885. Introduced to the world at Britain's main cycling show, the Stanley Cycle Show in London, it featured two wheels that were nearly equal in size, solid tyres and direct steer forks of the type still used today. The next model, which arrived in 1888, not only had two equally sized 66cm (26in) wheels but also featured John Boyd Dunlop's innovative pneumatic tyres (*see* pp. 30–31).

Despite their instant popularity with the masses, Rover Safety Bicycles did not completely dominate the roads and were disparagingly dubbed 'dwarf machines', 'crawlers' and 'beetles' by riders of high-wheelers. Maybe there was some innate snobbery about a machine that made cycling much more accessible; the high-wheeler had been the preserve of the middle and upper classes, and the very idea of riding something that was considered 'safe' may have been unappealing to wealthy young men, happy to take risks on their ordinaries. By contrast, the Rover and its ilk were relatively cheap, having been mass produced in the factories of Birmingham, Coventry and Nottingham. The models on offer cost 14 guineas, still a significant sum when the average income was 14 shillings a week, but users received a credit for introducing new customers, and the scheme was eminently more affordable than purchasing a new bike outright and enabled less-wealthy people to start cycling.

The effect of the Rover on the cycling boom of the 1890s cannot be overestimated, and it was quickly copied by manufacturers across Britain, Europe and the USA. As the great Italian bicycle manufacturer Ernesto Colnago, born in 1854, said: 'All modern-day bicycle designers owe a huge debt to J.K. Starley and his vision. Starley's stroke of genius is an inspiration to us all.'

The design of the present day bicycle has remained much the same since John Kemp Starley designed the Rover Safety Bicycle, which revolutionised transportation. Because it was much lower and more stable than the 'ordinary' bicycle, it became known as the Safety Bicycle.

6 Step-through frame

Throughout the early evolution of the bicycle there was a general assumption that the gender of a cyclist would be male. Although some manufacturers did make modifications to their designs to better suit women, these ungainly and uncomfortable side-saddle machines were inherently difficult and dangerous to ride. It is perhaps little surprise, then, that the relatively few ladies who did venture out on the roads usually did so on tricycles, which were easier to mount, more stable and could accommodate the volume of a crinoline that female fashion demanded.

However, by the 1890s the bicycle began to assume an increasingly important socio-political role as the popularity of the comparatively cheap, safe and easy-to-ride Rover was rapidly exploited by two growing political movements: Suffragism and Socialism. As Susan B. Anthony, the American social reformer and feminist, so memorably remarked in an 1896 interview: 'Let me tell you what I think of bicycling. I think it has done more to emancipate women than anything else in the world. It gives women a feeling of freedom and self-reliance. I stand and rejoice every time I see a woman ride by on a wheel – the picture of free, untrammeled womanhood.'

Whether as a result of enlightened forward thinking or having spotted a huge potential market, cycling companies began to sit up and take notice. First off the mark was the US-based Smith National Cycle Company who, in 1888, produced the Ladies' Dart Bicycle with a 'drop' frame. This featured a lower crossbar that allowed a woman to mount her bicycle more easily, skirts and all. This was to prove a breakthrough year for women's cycling, during which Miss Harriet H. Mills on her Dart and the 50-strong membership of her newly formed women's cycling club – the first in the USA – rode in their loose skirts, riding hats and gloves through the streets of Washington DC. Women riding their Darts were also present in Baltimore that summer at the League of American Wheelmen's annual parade (the League had been established in 1880 in order to advocate for paved roads, the success of which ultimately led to the American highway system) – the first time women cyclists had attended the prestigious event.

So huge was the demand for the Dart that the Smith Company was unable to keep up. Enter the bizarrely named Psycho ladies' bicycle, which rolled off the production line at the Starley works in Coventry in 1889. With its step-through drop frame, it allowed a woman to mount her bicycle without the unseemly display of showing a leg or a petticoat that would occur if she attempted to straddle a traditional horizontal crossbar on a diamond frame. The enforced upright style of riding would also, the inventors were sure, ensure that no unnecessary 'physical stimulation' should occur.

This step-through or drop design has survived and is used for many women's bikes to this day. Where once the removal of the crossbar had potentially threatened the structural integrity of the step-through frame, meaning they were less robust than the diamond frames of male bikes, the use of modern materials such as carbon fibre has now rectified the weakness. Nor is the step-through confined to women's bikes – it is the design employed by the Dutch bike so prevalent on the streets of Amsterdam, and some BMXs have a step-through-style frame in order to reduce the possibility of painful injury if overturned.

More recent modifications aside, however, it was the Dart and, in particular, the Starley Psycho that first enabled women from all walks of life to enjoy the sense of freedom and self-reliance that cycling can bring.

The 'freedom machine' and the step-through frame liberated generations of women.

7 Mountain bike

Mountain, or off-road biking, in its most literal sense has been around as long as bikes, though as a recognised sport its history began much more recently.

Very few roads were paved in the 19th century when the early bikes were being developed, forcing riders to use dirt tracks or very bumpy highways, with those wishing to travel further afield going off-piste. Despite this, people did ride extraordinary distances given the terrain and unsuitability of their bicycles. One of the earliest recorded accounts of off-road biking describes how in 1896 the 'Buffalo Soldiers' of the 25th Bicycle Infantry Corps – a regiment of black enlisted men led by a white lieutenant – rode 1900 miles in 41 days across America to 'test most thoroughly the bicycle as a means of transportation for troops.'

Mountain bikes as we know them, however, didn't start to emerge until the mid-20th century, when cross-country riders began modifying existing bikes to tackle tougher off-road conditions and perform more tricks. Notable among these was the Vélo Cross Club Parisien (VCCP), a small group of cyclocross bikers from the outskirts of Paris, who in the first half of the 1950s adapted their bikes and developed a sport, complete with tricks and airs, that is extremely similar to modern-day mountain biking.

In 1953, an American off-road cycling enthusiast, John Finley Scott, created the first-ever prototype mountain bike, which he called a 'Woodsie', the term used for the English rough-stuff bikes that inspired his design. Based on a Schwinn World frame, the bike had balloon tyres (thick tyres that contain air at low pressure, which enabled them to cope with uneven surfaces) and derailleur gears. In 1960, Scott built a version that featured a custom-built Jeff Buttler frame, side-pull brakes, drop handlebars, a triple crankset, a five-sprocket freewheel, and rear and front derailleurs.

Inspired by what Buttler had done with his bike, in the 1970s a group of friends set out to ride the trails around Mount Tamalpais in California. Needing bikes that were equal to the task, they settled on 'clunkers' – balloon-tyred, one-speed bikes like the Schwinn Excelsior, which had first rolled off the production lines in the 1930s. The importance of this gathering of the Larkspur Canyon Gang (as it was known) wasn't really their bikes, however, but the fact that they referred to their bicycles as 'mountain bikes', to differentiate them from road bikes.

The first truly successful mountain bike was the Breezer, created by road-bike racer Joe Breeze in 1977. Built from the same kind of lightweight tubing and high-end components that were popular in road bikes, but beefed up with extra bracing, it was equipped with knobby tyres that could cope with the rough terrain, and 18 gears to help with the steep climbs. It laid the groundwork for the creation of the modern mountain bike, although production was very limited and the bikes he produced were mostly bought by fellow mountain bikers.

This issue of low-unit production was solved in the 1980s, when the ever-shrewd and ingenious Scott became one of the early investors in a business called MountainBikes, founded by bike racer Gary Fisher. Fisher bought mountain-bike frames from renowned frame-builder Tom Richey, modified them, then sold the finished bikes in their hundreds. He proved that the making, marketing and selling of mountain bikes was a genuine business proposition rather than just a niche hobby.

When big companies, such as Specialized and Univega, started making the bikes in the early 1980s, the production, design and popularity of mountain bikes really took off, and the sport has never looked back.

The 1953 'Woodsie' bike – the forerunner of the modern mountain bike. The 1953 model featured a Schwinn World diamond frame, thick tyres, flat handlebars, derailleur gears and cantilever **brakes.**

8 Cyclocross bike

Cyclocross developed in the late 19th century as a way for professional riders to maintain their fitness throughout the winter months. Combining rough terrain that encouraged bike-handling skills and short sections that required riders to carry their bikes and run, which stimulated circulation in frozen limbs, it was the ideal form of off-season training.

In those days, cyclocross bore more of a resemblance to athletic events such as the steeplechase or cross-country running, since riders were required to travel from town to town either on- or off-road, negotiating permanent obstacles along the way, rather than racing around circuits featuring man-made hurdles, bridges and stairs.

By 1902, however, when the first national cyclocross championships (organised by Daniel Gousseau, a French soldier) were held in France, racing had moved on to circuits that featured both natural and man-made obstacles. After road racer Octave Lapize attributed his 1910 Tour de France win to his off-season cyclocross training, the sport spread beyond France to Belgium and Switzerland, as well as Luxembourg, Spain and Italy. The first international race was held in Paris in 1924.

Over the next few decades cyclocross went from strength to strength; not even the outbreak of World War II could halt its progress, with riders coming up with innovative ways to carry on, such as holding races in the streets of Montmartre in Paris, utilising the flights of stairs that lead up to the Sacré-Coeur. As it evolved, the early French domination of the sport was soon eclipsed by the 'Flahutes', the hard men of Belgium, so-called because they enjoyed nothing better than to race hard on the worst terrain and in the most appalling weather imaginable. Greatest of all these Belgians was Erik De Vlaeminck, brother of 'Mr Paris–Roubaix' Roger, who dominated the scene in the 1960s. Known as the 'Monarch of the Mud', De Vlaeminck was the Eddy Merckx of cyclocross, winning every world championship – bar the one of 1967, when he had trouble with his bike and was forced to withdraw – between 1966 and 1973.

It may have evolved from the tough, heavy touring bikes of the early 1900s, noted for their ability to cope with rough terrain, but since the creation of the racing bike in the late 1930s, the cyclocross bike has followed the design of its roadworthy cousin with only minor (but important) modifications. Dedicated cyclocross bikes began to appear in the 1950s and 1960s, although they remained virtually indistinguishable from standard road bikes, which at the time featured good clearance between tyres and frame, ideal for cyclocross as mud was less likely to stick to tyres and clog brakes and gears. Cantilever brakes with outward-facing arms and a straddle wire became popular as they gave better clearance and stopping power in muddy conditions than calliper brakes.

As cyclocross bikes developed in tandem with touring bikes, models were fitted with smaller chain rings to provide lower gears that were more suitable for coping with the slower speeds and obstacles of the sport. The introduction of lightweight materials such as carbon fibre and aluminium in the 1980s and 1990s also proved ideal, since the sport frequently required the rider to dismount and carry his machine – a skill known as 'portage'.

Frame geometry has also been adjusted over the years to allow for greater mud clearance for derailleurs and brakes, meaning that components don't jam or fail. Although knobby tyres have been around since the 1950s cyclocross bikes have also borrowed from the sport of mountain biking by adopting disc brakes for superior all-weather braking.

With its disc brakes and lightweight frame, the
cyclocross bike is well suited to cross-terrain
riding. Competitors tackle a hill climb during the
Men's U23 Pro race during the Cyclocross
National Championships in Connecticut, USA.

⑨ Eddy Merckx's hour record bike

The history of the hour record – the simple formulation that pits a lone rider against the clock for 60 minutes of lung-busting and leg-breaking effort as he pedals the greatest possible distance – is a long and illustrious one. However, few attempts are as memorable as that of Eddy Merckx, 'The Cannibal', at the Augustin Melgar Velodrome, Mexico City on 25 October, 1972.

The first ratified hour record was set by Henri Desgrange, the father of the Tour de France, who rode 35.325km (21.95 miles) at the Buffalo velodrome in Paris on 11 May, 1893. For the next 50 years, the event remained the preserve of the great track stars of the day, until the legendary Italian *campionissimo* (champion of champions) Fausto Coppi broke the record at the iconic Velodromo Vigorelli in Milan in 1942. This stood for 14 years, until it was broken by Jacques Anquetil (an outstanding time-triallist and the first man to win the Tour de France five times) in 1956 and 1967.

In the early 1970s, Merckx, the greatest all-rounder the sport has ever seen, considered the Vigorelli for his own attempt. It would, after all, allow for a direct comparison between his achievement and that of his illustrious predecessors. However, a visit to Milan in early October 1968 had proved disappointing – the track was waterlogged and unusable. Merckx would have to look elsewhere.

A few years previously, in 1968, Danish cyclist Ole Ritter had added over 500m (547 yards) to the existing record distance, in Mexico City – a feat that opened the eyes of the cycling community to the possibilities of altitude. Though the lack of oxygen presented its own problems, the lower resistance offered by the thinner air meant that less physical effort was required to achieve and maintain optimal speed. Merckx therefore opted to make his attempt there, and prepared for the low oxygen levels by training while hooked up to an air tank that replicated Mexico City's rarefied atmosphere.

The last piece of the jigsaw was the bike that would take Merckx to a new record of 49.431km (30.71 miles). Engineered by Ernesto Colnago, founder of the illustrious Colnago bicycle company, it was a miracle of feather-weight engineering. Faced with the challenge of producing a super-light time-trial bike capable of carrying the 1.85m (6ft 1in) tall, 72kg (159lb or 11 stone 5lb) Belgian – a rider capable of generating colossal power – at a sustained speed for 60 minutes, the Italian recalled later, 'I lightened everything; the cranks, drilled out the chain, because we wanted the lightest material and well, you couldn't buy a Regina Extra chain with holes drilled in it!'. The tubular tyres used for the attempt, the Clement number 1 Pista, weighed 90g (3.17oz) for the front wheel and 110g (3.9oz) for the rear.

In addition to these modifications, the bike's components were meticulously prepared and assembled. It was all worth it though, and at 5.5kg (12.1lb) it was the lightest bike ever used to set the hour record – by comparison, Bradley Wiggins' Pinarello Bolide, on which he set the 2016 record of 54.526km (33.88 miles), weighed in at the UCI minimum of 6.8kg (14.99lb), though it was considerably more aerodynamic than Merckx's machine.

Colnago watched the attempt from the middle of the velodrome, armed with everything he needed to make on-the-spot repairs. When the hour was up, Merckx collapsed on Colnago's shoulder. 'He said, "basta, enough ... that's the last time I'll ever do the hour record. The pain was incredible..."' Colnago remembered. 'But then he felt better and shook my hand and said "thank you" and that meant everything to me.' Having beaten the record by 700m (765 yards), Merckx never rode the hour again.

Eddy Merckx smashes the hour record at the Olympic Velodrome in Mexico City in 1972 on his super-light Colnago bike, setting the record at 49.431km.

10 Graeme Obree's 'Old Faithful'

'Old Faithful' – the bike on which Graeme Obree broke Francesco Moser's hour record in 1993 – is a DIY masterpiece of engineering, innovation and sheer ingenuity. Where Moser had used double-disc wheels and the best technology available to cycle a distance of 51.151km (31.8 miles), the relatively unknown Scotsman used a bike he built himself using found, salvaged and repurposed materials.

Obree had broken the British hour record in 1988 using a unique tucked position on a standard bike with the handlebars flipped upside down. Borrowing the position from downhill skiers, he rested his chest on his forearms and kept his knees as close together as possible, lowering his frontal area and reducing aerodynamic drag by around 15 per cent. He developed his bike as a response to the challenges this riding position threw up, using a narrower bottom bracket that challenged conventional bicycle geometry, a problem he solved with an oval tube from a tandem, which he turned sideways. The seat stem was salvaged from what his bike-shop colleagues called 'pishrust tubing' (slang for something rubbish and prone to rusting) from a BMX. Most famously, he used bearings from an old washing machine.

Despite its patchwork construction, Obree had faith in his machine, writing in his book *The Flying Scotsman*: 'I knew my baby had soul and I could not help going to the measured 10-mile TT course and ripping round, full-on.' The stage was thus set for his hour record attempt in Haimar, Norway. Intrigued by his home-made bike, journalists were keen to know more about the Scotsman's unconventional machine, asking questions that prompted Obree to reply on the day he broke the record that she was his 'Old Faithful' – and the name stuck.

In fact, Obree had made his first attempt the previous day, on a replica bike built with help from Mike Burrows, the man who had designed the revolutionary Lotus monocoque bike that Chris Boardman had ridden to a pursuit gold medal in the Barcelona Olympics in 1992. However, the first attempt failed, so Obree switched bikes, ate lots of marmalade sandwiches and the next day, on 17 July, 1993, rode 'Old Faithful' to set his mark of 51.596km (31.8 miles), a distance broken just a week later by Chris Boardman.

In 1993 and 1994, Obree used the same tuck position to become world individual pursuit and British time-trial champion. However, where many in the cycling world recognised a maverick innovator, the Union Cycliste International (UCI) saw only a threat to the perceived purity of the sport, where technological advantage trumped human endeavour, and promptly banned the tuck position. In response, Obree then developed the 'superman' – riding with arms fully extended – which he used to take the hour record again on 27 April, 1994 with a distance of 52.713km (32.75 miles). However, the UCI banned that position too. A career as a professional road rider beckoned when the Scotsman signed for the new Le Groupement team on 1 January, 1995, but allegedly, because Obree refused to take performance-enhancing drugs, he was quietly dropped from his squad.

Despite this major setback in his career, Obree's thirst for pushing the boundaries remains undimmed. In 2013 he powered the 'Beastie', a bicycle ridden in the prone position, to a new world record, achieving speeds of 91kph (56.5mph). True to form, the Beastie was built in Obree's kitchen using a saucepan as a shoulder support and parts salvaged from old bicycles and roller skates, alongside major innovations inside the shell, such as push-pull levers.

Graeme Obree's manager Vic Haines shouts words
of encouragement to him as he races towards a new
hour record in 1993, setting it at 51.151km. Graeme
Obree's 'Old Faithful' was a DIY masterpiece of
engineering, innovation and ingenuity.

11   Chris Froome's Pinarello Dogma

The Pinarello Dogma F8 that Chris Froome rode to his second Tour de France title in 2016 is the perfect example of what can be achieved when all the evolutionary gains of the last 100 years coalesce in one brilliant machine.

The family firm Pinarello began manufacturing bikes on a small scale in Catena di Villorba, Italy, in the 1920s, but it was Giovanni Pinarello – a *maglia nera* in 1951 (the black jersey once awarded to the last-placed rider) in the Giro d'Italia – who brought the brand to prominence.

Following the end of his own cycling career in 1952 Pinarello invested in his own company, Pinarello bikes, which manufactured bikes and sold them from a store that opened in Treviso that same year. He also, crucially, sponsored amateur cycling teams, something that greatly promoted the bikes and the store.

This continued until 1960, when the company sponsored its first professional team, the Mainetti, which developed many local champions. In 1966 the team achieved its first major victory when Guido de Rosso won the Tour d'Avenir in France and put the company on the cycling map. By the 1970s, the bikes were being used to score wins at the Grand Tours, with the victory of Fausto Bertoglio at the 1975 Giro d'Italia proving an especially big boost to Pinarello's international reputation.

In 1984, American Alexi Grewal rode to Olympic gold on a Pinarello, bringing the bikes to the attention of the US market. However, it was Miguel Induráin's unbeaten streak of five consecutive Tour de France wins in the 1990s that cemented the brand's popularity. Pinarello was also at the forefront of the carbon-fibre revolution, designing and creating increasingly extraordinary time-trialling machines, including Induráin's iconic hour record bike and the Chrono Indu on which he won both the Tour de France and the Giro d'Italia in 1993.

This innovation in materials had been sparked in the 1980s when Giovanni Pinarello's son Fausto joined the company and started exploring the uses of magnesium as a frame-building material. Combining the comfort of steel with the handling of carbon, Pinarello's magnesium Dogmas quickly became a favourite with consumers, but the manufacturing process was difficult and they were prone to corrosion.

With cyclists seeking ever-lighter bikes, the material of choice for road bikes became carbon fibre, which boasts an unbeatable strength-to-weight ratio, allowing larger, more aerodynamic tubes. And it's aerodynamics, not weight, that make a huge difference on those flat and rolling stages – in a test conducted by *Cycling Weekly* in 2015 they discovered that, for a cyclist generating 200 watts, an aerodynamic carbon-fibre bike was nearly 2kph (1.24mph) faster than a standard lightweight one.

These technical innovations, together with Pinarello's reputation and proven track record, have made them one of the most respected brands in cycling. Still a relatively small company, the bikes are used exclusively by members of Team Sky in professional races, which means Pinarello can provide a rapid and specific response to the team's changing demands. And it's easy to see why Team Sky uses them. The carbon Dogma, for instance, is equipped with drag-reducing forks and an aerofoil seat-post to make the bike as aerodynamic as possible – the Dogma claims to be 40 per cent more aerodynamically efficient than its competitors as well as being lighter and yet stiffer (for improved bike handling) than almost any bike on the market.

The Pinarello Dogma F8 is the culmination of
100 years of cycling evolution. Chris Froome,
shown here, taking part in a training ride in
Monaco on the bike that he would ride to
victory in the 2016 Tour de France.

The Gear

12 Pneumatic tyres

The invention of the pneumatic tyre pre-dates the creation of either the bicycle or the car. Often erroneously attributed to John Dunlop, whose tyres were more accurately a re-invention, the first patent for pneumatic tyres, known as 'aerial wheels', was filed by another Scotsman, Robert William Thomson, in 1845.

Thomson, who taught himself chemistry, astronomy and electrical engineering, was only 23 when he applied for UK patent number 10990 for the invention that would eventually have a huge impact on bicycles and, later, cars. However, since neither of these vehicles had been invented in 1847, when the first model was demonstrated to the public, Thomson's pneumatic tyre was mounted on a horse-drawn cart and pulled around London's Regent's Park.

Consisting of an inflated canvas tube inside a leather casing, the aerial wheel established the principle of the pneumatic tyre – using an inflated, air-cushioned tube to provide a smoother, more comfortable and much quieter ride. Moreover, one set was recorded as lasting for 1200 miles without showing any signs of deterioration. However, despite their obvious benefits, aerial wheels proved too difficult and costly to make and Thomson duly returned to making solid rubber tyres – alongside other inventions such as an invalid chair with rubber tyres, and new commercial machinery for sugar production. It would be another 40 years before technology and the availability of thinner rubber caught up with the ideas behind Thomson's invention, though by this time the story would start not with four wheels, but with three.

John Boyd Dunlop was a Scottish veterinarian who had relocated from Scotland to Belfast in 1867. Watching his son labour over the cobbles on his tricycle he was inspired to invent – or re-invent – the pneumatic tyre in a bid, as reports variously suggest, to save his son from constant headaches or a sore behind. In developing his pneumatic tyres, Dunlop made use of vulcanised rubber – a process credited to Charles Goodyear in 1844 that removed the sulphur from rubber, rendering it both waterproof and flexible – and advertised his tyres for the first time in the *Irish Cyclist* in 1888. The bicycle boom was at its height when Irish cycling champion Willie Hume purchased a set of Dunlops for his bike the following year, becoming the first ever rider to use pneumatic tyres in competition and, it's said, never losing a race when riding on them.

A middlingly successful rider previously, Hume's success lit the fuse for Dunlop's success. Thomson's original patent having lapsed, Dunlop's 1888 patent for the pneumatic tyre laid the groundwork for a company whose success continues today. It's interesting to note, however, that Dunlop originally patented a bicycle tyre – it was the Michelin brothers, Édouard and André, who were the first to use pneumatic tyres on a car, in 1895.

In a nice twist of fate, at the start of the Giro d'Italia 2014 in Belfast the opening team time-trial passed the site of the old North of Ireland Cricket Club grounds, where Willie Hume won his first race on the revolutionary pneumatic tyres that had such an impact on the sport's history.

Women at work inserting wires into tyres at the Dunlop Pneumatic Tyre factory in Coventry, UK, in 1896. One of the great innovations in bicycle design, the pneumatic tyre actually predates the bike and the car.

13 Tubular tyres

Although pneumatic tyres were an immediate success with professional riders, it was a Frenchman, Édouard Michelin, who pushed tyre technology further, developing something approximating the first of the three main types of pneumatic tyre – clincher, tubular and wired – that are grouped according to how they are attached to the wheel.

The clincher-style tyre hooks onto the wheel rim and is inflated by a separate inner tube. This is still the standard tyre for general bike users. However, those early Michelin tyres were heavy and even in the late 1800s professional riders were looking for every advantage. They turned, therefore, to the tubular tyre – a vulcanised or hand-made cloth casing stitched around an inner tube and then glued to the wheel rim – which could be inflated to a much higher pressure, handled far better and was considerably lighter than the Michelin clincher tyre. Professionals also claimed that these 'tubulars' gave a more comfortable ride and greater traction than the 'clinchers'.

A great deal of myth and folklore quickly attached to the gluing and curing of tubular tyres and the impact these had on performance. For instance, when Gino Bartali won the Tour de France in 1938 after a spectacular display in the Alps, his success was attributed to tubular tyres that had been stored in a cool, dry cellar for two years before the race.

The tubular tyre – also known as a sew-up in the USA or a *boyau* in French (after the name for a sausage casing) – has remained the industry standard for bike racing. The best-quality ones are created by spinning fine thread on a drum and then coating it in latex. The higher the TPI (threads per inch) the better, and the highest TPI is more flexible, stronger and lighter (and, inevitably, more expensive). Parallelograms of the material are then cut and folded around a thin rubber tube to create the tyre. They are less prone to 'pinch flats' because the tyre is glued into a groove on the wheel rim rather than being clinched in place against the metal rim. Pinch flats are caused by the tube being 'pinched' or caught between the rim and the tyre if the rider hits a sharp object.

There are, however, disadvantages associated with the use of tubulars. The most important of these is that they are difficult to repair once punctured, necessitating riders without team support to carry spares. In addition, improperly glued tubulars can simply roll off the rim, causing serious crashes. For just this reason, Spaniard Miguel Induráin – the first rider to win five successive Tours de France (1991–1995) – would regularly switch to clincher tyres when descending.

Clincher tyre technology has improved significantly, however, so that the rolling friction and aerodynamics of a clincher tyre are comparable to tubulars. Tubeless clinchers have crossed over from mountain biking, where they gained popularity because they do away with the need for an inner tube. In addition to the advantage of incurring fewer pinch flats, and a tubular will also allow a cyclist to keep riding with a puncture until a support vehicle arrives with a spare wheel. Tubeless clincher tyres are still popular with professional cyclists.

Essentially, the choice of tubular or clincher boils down to what riders wish to do, the terrain, budget and personal preference, although among aficionados the romance of tubulars remains. A tubular wheelset maintains a weight advantage over a clincher wheelset because the rims don't need to be as robust to withstand the high internal pressures of a clincher. The ability to run tubular tyres at very low and high pressures means they are the tyre of choice for cyclocross and track cycling.

Gino Bartali celebrating his first
Tour de France victory in 1938.
Bartali won the race using tubular
tyres which remain the tyre of choice
for the elite cyclist.

14 Spokes

Without wheels there would be no bicycles. And without spokes, we would still be riding on wagon wheels.

In 1869, Frenchman Eugène Meyer attempted to patent his latest invention – a wire-spoked wheel for the 'ordinary' or vélocipède bicycle that held the spokes in tension at the hub flange in the middle by use of brass nuts, rather than heavy wooden spokes held in compression that had been used on the hobby horse. Sadly for Meyer, the patent was not granted because he had made the mistake of selling a pair of his hand-crafted wheels before the patent was issued, invalidating it completely and resulting in his name fading from the annals of bicycling history.

Instead, it was James Starley and William Hillman who got the credit when, in August 1870, the Coventry bicycle manufacturers were granted a patent for their 'improvement to vélocipède wheels'. They then went on to create the Ariel, which sported the first long-lasting, lightweight tension wheels on a commercially produced bicycle.

James Moore, the British cycling champion, was one of Starley's first customers. What Starley (and Meyer before him) had devised was truly revolutionary – the tensioned wire spokes had an element of shock absorption that made the ride altogether more comfortable, and the wheels themselves could also be much larger, which greatly increased the distance travelled per revolution of the wheel. The best part, however, was the reduction in the wheel's weight, and it's that which attracted Moore, one of Britain's first great bike racers, to Starley's workshops.

Starley's Ariel wheel had one major flaw, though: the spokes were mounted in pairs, so they couldn't be individually tensioned to ensure the wheel ran true. In response to this, in December the same year (1870), William Grout of the Tension Bicycle Works in Stoke Newington, London, patented what would become the modern tension spoke. Grout would also invent the forerunner of the folding bicycle – a penny-farthing with a front wheel that split into four and packed away into 'Grout's Wonderful Bag'.

A few years later, in 1874, Starley reacted by producing the 'triple cross' tangential spoking pattern – so-called because each spoke crosses three others – an innovation that remains the standard today. By angling individual spokes, setting them off at a tangent to the hub and almost at right angles to each other, the tangents on either side of the wheels could be balanced to produce a more rigid, robust wheel that allowed power to be transferred more efficiently from pedal to wheel rim. Moreover, since the spokes could be individually tensioned, the wheel could be quickly and easily adjusted and stayed true.

Spoked wire wheels soon caught on with manufacturers, and by 1878 the Surrey Machinist Company were advertising their Invincible model with a whopping 300 spokes per wheel. Starley licensed his tangent-spoked wheels to bicycle makers Jefferis and Haynes, charging them five shillings a pair and an additional 10 shillings when a completed bicycle, called 'The Tangent', was sold.

Moreover, since the spoking system made wire wheels much stronger, it was soon adopted by the automotive and aerospace industries and used for the wheels of motorbikes, cars and planes for many decades. Today, although most cars, planes and bikes use alternative systems, many non-professional bikes are still fitted with tangent-spoked wheels.

James Starley and William Hillman's Ariel defined the features of the 'ordinary' bicycle. Such large wheels were only achievable with the invention of tensioned wire spokes that allowed the rigid and robust wheel to stay true.

15 Quick-release skewer

A quick-release skewer is the mechanism used for removing and attaching a bicycle wheel that is still used today. To better understand why its invention was necessary, we need to understand how cyclists had to change gears in the days before the invention of the derailleur (*see pp. 40–41*).

Early racing bicycles were equipped with double-sided rear hubs, with up to two cogs on each side. To change gears, a rider had to stop, dismount, remove the wing nut from the rear wheel, flip the latter round so it engaged with a different cog, secure the wheel with the wing nut and finally ride away. Not surprisingly, deciding when to make a gear change became one of the most crucial aspects of racing and getting it wrong could easily cost riders a spot on the podium.

And it was just such a loss – or so legend has it – that inspired the invention of the quick-release mechanism. In 1927, a young Italian rider named Tullio Campagnolo took part in the Gran Premio della Vittoria, one of Italy's premier races for amateur riders. Campagnolo was going well and challenging for the win until he was forced to change gears and, fumbling with the rear wing nut in the snowy conditions and unable to remove his rear wheel, he lost all chance of success. '*Bisogna cambiare qualcosa de drio*' ('something needs changing at the back') declared the disappointed rider. Vowing to develop a better solution, the young Italian worked hard and, three years later, patented the quick-release skewer in 1930.

Ever since, this brilliantly simple piece of cycling kit has benefitted cyclists, whether they are changing a wheel on a commute or in the heat of a race. Where a wing nut may work itself loose over time or prove frustratingly stubborn to unscrew, a quick-release skewer, which works by tensioning a rod that runs through the hollow axle and grabbing on to a nut on the other side, does not. The tension is released by simply flipping open a lever, making the removal of the wheel a piece of cake. Generations of cyclists have good reason to thank Tullio Campagnolo for inventing this elegant and simple solution.

Except that he didn't. According to research by the bicycle historian David Herlihy, published in the 2014 *Bicycle Quarterly*, no copy of a quick-release mechanism patent exists at the Campagnolo head offices. Moreover, the only snowy Gran Premio took place in 1925, not 1927, and Campagnolo isn't mentioned as being a favourite in any of the race reports for the entire decade. The patents Campagnolo did file relating to the quick-release mechanism were for improvements to an existing design, but there simply is no original patent for the quick-release skewer that is said to date from 1930. Campagnolo's true genius, *Bicycle Quarterly* argues, lay in taking and improving upon the ideas of others to provide racers with new innovations, including the quick-release skewer.

The innovative quick-release skewer revolutionised fast wheel changes. Valentino Campagnolo, son of Tulio Campagnolo, shown here at the headquarters of the company.

Chain

What truly made the safety bicycle the prototype of the modern bike: the equal-sized wheels? The diamond geometry of the frame? Or the bicycle chain?

Phenomenally popular as it briefly was in the late 1870s and 1880s, the 'ordinary' bicycle suffered one huge limitation. By attaching the pedals directly to the front wheel, the top speed was limited by the size of that wheel. The bigger the diameter, the greater the distance covered by one revolution of the wheel. Thus manufacturers could either produce ever-larger front wheels – and some did – or find another solution.

The idea of a chain drive that allowed the transfer of the force a rider exerted on the pedal to turn the wheels had been mooted in the late 1860s in both France and Britain, and several patents were filed at that time. The simple block chain – comprised of two plates, a pin and small steel blocks – is both rugged and easy to produce, and it quickly gained popularity with track riders. However, it was the bush roller chain that would be used for all other bicycles, and is still in common use today.

Both types of chain were invented by Hans Renold, a Swiss engineer who was working in Manchester in the 1880s. The roller design significantly reduced friction by linking a series of short cylindrical rollers with side links to form a chain that was then mounted on a toothed cog or sprocket. This combination of chain and sprocket was the chain drive that J.K. Starley would incorporate in his safety bicycles from 1886 onwards, after his uncle James had first road-tested the Renold chain in a series of popular tricycles.

It was while they were being used on tricycles, however, that the major problem with chain drives came to light: poor road and weather conditions could leave them fouled with mud and damaged by increased wear and tear on the mechanism. Tricycle riders were thus advised to clean and oil their chains regularly, although this was unpopular since the lubricant transferred easily to a rider's clothes. J. Harrison Carter's patented Oil-tight Chain Lubricator and Gear Cover was one early solution to the problem and the chain case became a popular accessory, particularly on women's bicycles.

In 1879 Henry J. Lawson borrowed the new chain-drive technology pioneered by James Starley's tricycles for his Bicyclette safety bicycle. Although the bike never caught the public's imagination and retained a larger front wheel (unlike Starley's safety bikes), the name 'bicyclette' was adopted by the French as a general term used to describe a safety-style bicycle. Another bike that made use of the chain drive was the 1884 Kangaroo, a so-called 'dwarf' high-wheeler-style bicycle made by Hillman, Herbert and Cooper, whose geared chain drive allowed a radical reduction in the size of the front wheel (although pitching head first over the handlebars was still a distinct possibility for riders).

And then came the Rover in the mid-1880s. By using a chain drive mounted on a sprocket, Starley was able to change the gear differential of the rear wheel of his new design so it rotated as if it had a diameter of 127cm (50in), though its actual diameter was only 76.2cm (30in). This allowed Starley to radically reduce the size of the Rover's front wheel without any loss of speed, a drastic modification that, together with the bike's revolutionary drive chain, ensured the days of the ordinary were over.

The bicycle chain was first introduced by
James Starley for his popular tricycles,
and the 1879 Bicyclette (central left) and
the 1884 Kangaroo (central right) both
used a chain drive in their design.

Kirkpatrick Bicycle, 1839.

Phantom Bicycle, 1869.

Bicyclette, 1879.

Kangaroo Bicycle, 1884.

Otto Dicycle, 1881.

"Rudge," 1884.

17 Simplex derailleur

The derailleur is one of the most iconic inventions in the history of bicycle design. Taking its name from the French verb *dérailler* – literally 'to derail' – it is a system of rods and pulleys that moves the bicycle chain from one sprocket to another, allowing the rider to automatically change gear on a moving bicycle. Its effect on the development of modern cycle racing cannot be understated: the average speed of races jumped sharply and it's said that the last rider to finish the 1937 Tour averaged the same speed as that of the winner in 1936.

The first true derailleur was patented by Parisian Jean Loubeyre in 1895. Operated by a rod attached to the chain and controlled by a lever located near the saddle, the system offered the rider two speeds. In 1896, Englishman Edmund Hodkinson patented his Gradient three-speed gear-changing system, operated by the rider pedalling backwards to lift the chain, moving the cog and then forward pedalling to re-engage the chain. Simple and effective, this gear-shifting method was successfully in production by 1899. In 1905, Paul de Vivie – a passionate cyclotouriste – manufactured a four-speed derailleur known as Le Chemineau.

However, these new gearing systems encountered considerable opposition from some cyclists, including the originator of the Tour de France, Henri Desgrange, who wrote in *L'Équipe*: 'variable gears are only for people over forty-five. Isn't it better to triumph by the strength of your muscles than by the artifice of a derailleur? We are getting soft. As for me, give me a fixed gear!'

In 1928, a French bike-shop owner in Dijon introduced the Simplex, a design by Lucien Juy that allowed for ultra-precise gear shifting, thanks to a 'plunger' system – whereby a pulley was used to tension the chain while two guide plates moved it to a different sprocket. This assembly was moved sideways by a push-rod with a chain running through its centre. The entire device worked against a tensioned spring. Its fast gear shifting proved enormously popular and by 1933 Juy claimed he was making 40,000 per year, and dominating the market. Juy marketed the Simplex by sponsoring the star riders of the day to use his derailleur rather than those from rival companies.

After the war came the real game-changer – the Campagnolo Gran Sport of 1949. This was the first derailleur to perfect the parallelogram design, which consisted of two parallel arms that swung the lower body from side to side. This allowed it to be mounted at a 90-degree angle so it moved clear of the wheel and could drop out smoothly when the mechanism was activated.

The parallelogram derailleur is the blueprint for every modern gear shifter and was quickly adopted by other manufacturers, not least Simplex. Once the biggest manufacturers of derailleurs in the world, Simplex had lost out to Campagnolo's innovations so, in 1962, Lucien Juy decided to manufacture his parallelogram derailleurs from the new wonder material – plastic. Not content with limiting the use of polyoxymethylene to certain parts of his Simplex Prestige, the entire unit was now made of the new thermoplastic, known for its stiffness, low friction and stability, a step that was bold, forward thinking – and completely disastrous. Because it was made of plastic it was prone to cracking if poorly maintained, and Simplex's reputation for quality was wiped out at a stroke.

Currently, 90% of the professional peloton use electronic gear shifters. In 2014, Baron BioSystems announced the Automated Bike Shifting system, which utilises user-generated data to determine optimum gear choice. The BioShift is still in its infancy, but it may not be long before we see pro riders with fully automated shifting systems.

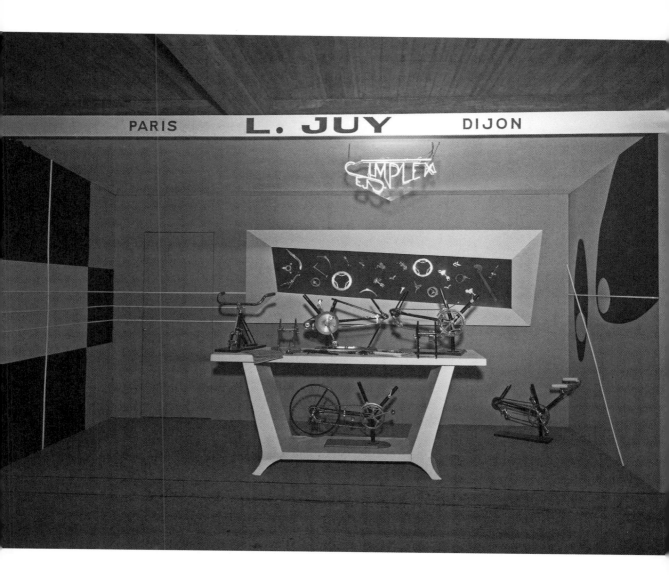

The innovative Simplex derailleur allowed riders to automatically shift gears without having to dismount their bike and remove the rear wheel. Here, a Simplex trade stand at an exhibition in Brussels, Belgium, circa 1955, displaying Simplex bicycle products.

18 Freewheel or *roue libre*

The basic drivetrain of a bicycle consists of a pair of pedals and two toothed wheels or sprockets mounted on the rear wheel connected directly to the chain. The earliest pedal-propelled bicycles were fixed wheel (or 'fixie') machines with the sprockets attached directly to the back wheel, so their riders would pedal backwards to come to a controlled stop. The problem with this is that on a fast descent, for example, it's impossible for your legs to keep up with the speed of your pedals and also to brake, because you can't pedal backwards.

The solution to this lay in allowing the back wheel to rotate faster than the pedals, allowing a rider to safely navigate downhill by coasting along with their feet still on the pedals. The freewheel – or *roue libre* – is a simple mechanical device that features a finger-like intendations pawls. It works like a cable tie. The end will move freely through the loop in one direction but the tiny pawls stop it from being pulled free from the opposite direction when tightened. Beautifully simple and effective, the freewheel helps a rider conserve energy and prevents the risk of accidents at high speed by allowing them to coast along safely.

First patented in 1869 by William Van Anden of Poughkeepsie, New York, the single-ratchet device didn't catch on initially. It wasn't until the advent of the safety bicycle and the pneumatic tyre in the 1880s that the value of the freewheel began to capture bicycle designers' imaginations, going on to impact two important areas of bicycle technology: braking and gearing.

If a cyclist were to make use of the benefits of free-wheeling, or coasting, then they needed an efficient braking system to replace the act of pedalling backwards. The American solution, developed in the 1890s, was the coaster (or drum) brake (*see* pp. 54–55), which teamed the freewheel with an in-hub back-pedal brake that made stopping easier and safer using friction. The British solution was the calliper (or rim) brake (*see* pp. 52–53) fitted on the front handlebar. In terms of gearing, by 1897, Ernst Sachs of Germany was successfully marketing a freewheel that temporarily lessened the load on the bicycle chain, potentially allowing it to be smoothly shifted between different sprockets. By increasing the number of sprockets, a rider could choose between different gear ratios, making riding uphill less of a chore. Until the development of the hub (*see* pp. 44–45) and derailleur gears (*see* pp. 40–41), this involved manually moving the chain from one sprocket to another.

The freewheel quickly became popular, allowing commuters and cyclotourists to ride at speed and over long distances and save energy. But not everyone was a fan. Following the 1912 Tour de France the ever-irascible Henri Desgrange wrote in *L'Auto*: 'Over the 379km of stage eleven, the riders applied pressure on the pedals for scarcely half the distance. The rest was covered freewheeling.' However, it was a French company, Le Cyclo, that developed the idea of the freewheel as a gearing device by incorporating a two-sprocket version that could be screwed onto a threaded hub, in 1924. Six years later they introduced a four-sprocket freewheel, soon adding a triple chainring that allowed a rider to select between 12 gears. Front and rear derailleurs quickly followed.

Where once the freewheel was built directly into the gear assembly, which was then mounted on the hub, the freewheel mechanism is now generally fitted directly on the hub. BMX bikes, coaster bikes and unicycles are all examples of single-speed bikes with a freewheel mechanism. The freewheel ratchet is still a feature of the modern bicycle, its tick-tick-tick a reminder of the continued evolution of the bicycle and its storied past.

Brilliantly simple, the freewheel allows a rider to conserve energy and avoid high speed crashes. This poster shows a vintage Villiers freewheel from the 1930s.

PRINTED IN ENGLAND

THE
VILLIERS
MODEL DE LUXE
FREE WHEEL

MADE IN ENGLAND

TO UNS...

THE VILLIERS MODEL DE LUXE

RUNS ON ONE ROW OF LARGE BALLS

Sturmey-Archer 3-Speed Hub

As the safety bicycle with its two equal-sized wheels grew in popularity at the end of the 19th century, designers and inventors turned their attention to using gears to replicate the advantages of the 'ordinary's' larger front wheel.

When one turn of the pedals equals one turn of the wheel – known as direct drive – the 'ordinary', with its massive front wheel, had an obvious advantage on the flat. Climbing any sort of gradient was a different matter, however, and here the safety bicycle had the edge. The holy grail, therefore, was to create a system that allowed the rear wheel to spin a greater or fewer number of times for one turn of the pedals so that a rider could spin speedily on the flat and climb hills with relative ease.

With the introduction of the bicycle chain (*see* pp. 38–39), gearing became a possibility. By mounting a large-toothed cog wheel or sprocket on the cranks that attach to the pedals and coupling it to a smaller cog/sprocket on the rear wheel with a chain, the back wheel could make several revolutions for one turn of the pedals.

Where the continental solution to shifting gear went down the derailleur route, mounting differently sized sprockets in parallel on the rear wheel, British designers focused on the planetary or epicyclic gear. This utilises a fixed, central 'sun' gear attached directly to the axle and surrounded by a series of 'planet' cogs that roll smoothly around it. The planet gears mesh with an inside-out gear – with its teeth on the inside – called the annulus. The planets are held in place by a cage and it fits inside a sprocket mounted in the metal drum-like bicycle hub.

How the annulus and the cage interact with the sprocket determines the gear ratio. In a low gear the sprocket drives the annulus, which drives the planet cage, which then turns the hub, lowering the gear by around 20 per cent. In a high gear, this is reversed, with the sprocket driving the planet cage and the annulus driving the hub, increasing the gear by around 25 per cent. In middle gear or direct drive, the sprocket drives the hub directly.

The epicyclic gear itself was nothing new – its history goes back to the 2nd century AD, when Ptolemy used epicyclic gear trains to predict planetary movement. Bicycle manufacturers began experimenting with it in tricycles during the 1870s, but it was an 1895 patent granted to Seward Thomas Johnson of Indiana, USA, for a simple two-speed hub gear that really set the ball rolling. Three years later, a perfected version, known simply as 'The Hub', became the first commercially produced compact hub gear. Small and light, extremely durable, low maintenance and easy to use as cyclists rode along, the hub gear was hailed as the future for variable gearing.

Its inventor was William Reilly of Salford, England, and the hugely successful three-speed hub gear he designed should really bear his name. Unfortunately for Reilly, he had signed a restrictive contract with his employers and was unable to file the patent under his own name. Instead, bicycle manufacturer James Archer filed it for him in August 1901, 11 days after Henry Sturmey – cycling journalist, technical editor and motorcar designer – patented a similar design.

When Raleigh bought both patents in 1902, they initially put Archer/Reilly's patent into production as the superior design, although Sturmey was the more famous name. Bitterly disappointed at this, Sturmey threatened to take his patent to a rival manufacturer. Desperate to keep his name associated with the company, Raleigh agreed to market their 3-Speed Hub as the Sturmey-Archer, although neither man was actually involved in the design. Reilly was written out of cycling history, earning just 1 per cent of the royalties for his trouble.

The iconic Sturmey-Archer 3-Speed Hub bought a simple and elegant gearing solution to mass production bicycles. This 1947 poster shows the full range of Sturmey-Archer 3- and 4-Speed Hubs.

20 Clipless pedals

It's an unmistakable sound – the 'click' as the peloton clips in before setting off for another day on the road – but it's also a relatively recent one.

The first patent for a clipless pedal was filed in 1895 by American Charles Hanson, but until the mid-1980s professional riders still traditionally used toe clips and straps to attach their cycling shoes to their pedals.

One rider and one pedal changed all that. In 1985, Frenchman Bernard Hinault rode to his fifth and final Tour de France victory using a pair of LOOK clipless pedals. The idea, borrowed from ski bindings, was simple and revolutionary – a triangular plastic cleat snapped securely into spring-loaded jaws – and could be released again with a flick of the foot.

The French-made LOOK system was safer than toe clips and straps in a crash, allowing a rider to quickly unclip from his pedals to avoid injury. This was a huge advance on the Italian-made Cinelli M71 that had debuted in 1970, a square-shaped metal device that locked the rider's shoe in place with a lever and that required manual release under normal circumstances. The M71 quickly became known jokingly as the 'death cleat', though it was actually no more perilous than using traditional toe straps since the lever was on the outside edge of the pedal so that in the event of the crash the action of the lever hitting the floor would release the rider's foot.

The LOOK clipless pedal was more comfortable and efficient too, though it was somewhat clunky. In addition the cleats, which attached the pedal to the sole of the shoe, forced the rider to adopt an ungainly totter when walking. But what the pedal lacked in looks it more than made up for in commercial and sporting success, becoming the first widely accepted three-hole mounting standard. The following year, American Greg LeMond would replicate his teammate's Tour de France victory using the same LOOK pedals.

Since the launch of the M71 and throughout the LOOK era, manufacturers in the USA, New Zealand, Italy and Germany tried to emulate the French company's success. In 1989, Richard Byrne, in the USA, had designed the first Speedplay pedal, introducing the revolutionary Speedplay X two years later. This double-sided, lollipop-shaped pedal was a radical departure from clipless pedals, allowing a rider to clip in to either side of the platform because the springs and tensioning mechanisms were housed in the cleat, not the pedal. Thanks to a lucky accident, the Speedplay owes its tiny size to the fact that Byrne had reproduced his blueprints on a printer that reduced their size to 77 per cent.

However, it was Japanese components' manufacturer Shimano who hit gold with their Shimano Pedal Dynamics (SPD) pedals and cleats. Originally developed in 1990 for the mountain-bike market, the SPD system uses a small cleat recessed into the sole of the shoe. Coupled with double-sided pedals, it is much easier to unclip and then walk around normally using SPD cleats than it is when wearing cleats that fitted the LOOK clipless pedal. So great has been the success of SPD in the commuter and casual cycling market that it's now possible to find SPD sandals and sneakers.

Allowing the seamless transfer of power from foot to pedal, clipless pedals were a revelation in bike riding. No longer would a rider have to tighten his toe straps before launching a vicious sprint or a stinging attack – the security of the clipless pedal meant the totality of his power went through the pedal stroke, into the bike and on to the road.

The revolutionary clipless pedal allowed the seamless transfer of power from foot to pedal. Bernard Hinault worked closely with French company LOOK on the design and used the LOOK clipless pedal as he rode to his final Tour de France victory in 1985, shown below.

21 Saddle

From the wooden plank seat of the Draisine to the featherweight, barely-there blades used by the professional peloton, the bicycle saddle has evolved considerably to improve both comfort and performance.

The saddle supplied with an 'ordinary' scarcely improved upon the Draisine's wooden plank, consisting of, at its most sophisticated, a ring of unpadded metal. However, the arrival of the safety bicycle, with its universal appeal to would-be cyclists, threw the design spotlight on the saddle.

Cue John Boultbee Brooks, a horse-saddle manufacturer who owned a leatherworks in Birmingham and was to play a critical role in the safety-bicycle revolution. In 1882, having been unimpressed by how hard the wooden seat of a bicycle was, he filed his first patent for the original sprung bicycle saddle. A range of designs followed, including the Bunker pneumatic (a kind of inflated ring with rudimentary nose, in 1892), the Bartlett pneumatic (featuring a series of air holes, in 1894) and the Bray's moveable (a saddle split into two adjustable halves, in 1898). This series of patented saddles standardised the design of the bicycle saddle – a slender nose allowing the legs to turn the pedals at high cadence and a wider seat area that supports the pelvis. The length allows for adjustment of the riding position and body weight when needed. Finished in leather over a sprung metal frame, the Brooks saddle is still manufactured in the traditional way in Birmingham today.

The rise in popularity of cycling with women during the 1890s resulted in the Christie Anatomical saddle – resembling two plump padded cushions mounted on a steel frame – which was specifically conceived to prevent women from 'overexciting' themselves and prevent the shocking prospect of any kind of sexual stimulation. Even medical practitioners supported it, as is evident from a statement by an unnamed (male) physician that: 'We have given a fair trial to this saddle, which is intended to do away with the ill-effects of pressure on the perineum and soft parts under the pubic arch.'

There are now several different types of saddle, but one feature common to all is the 'cradle'. Fashioned from steel or more lightweight materials, it attaches the saddle to the seat post and also determines the width and shape of the finished saddle – from narrow blades to the very padded comfort of the adjustable, articulated split 'Easy Seat' that has been around since 1982.

Today, saddles are generally composed of a hard, lightweight plastic shell that is padded and then covered with the material of choice. Gel saddles are popular with those looking for extra comfort and modern fabrics allow for better wicking of the moisture that can exacerbate saddle sores. Alternatively, leather is hardwearing and eventually moulds itself perfectly to a rider's buttocks.

Where weight is a consideration, for example in the peloton, the seat rails may be of carbon or titanium and padding on the saddle will often be minimal. Professional riders have very specific requirements for their saddles, depending on how much they move, their size and height. Fit and comfort over long distances is key, so no one rider will have exactly the same specifications. Companies like Cobb and ISM are now producing saddles that provide a more comfortable ride by easing pressure on the nerve bundles located in the crotch. The innovative ISM split nose saddle eases pressure on the rider's perineum to improve blood flow, while Cobb saddles all feature a relief channel that reduces numbing and saddle sores and relieves pressure from the hamstrings and the adductors.

From its evolution from the wooden plank via the horse saddle, the modern bicycle saddle now gives a much more comfortable ride. The iconic leather Brooks saddle, the forerunner of them all, is still made by hand in their factory in Birmingham, UK.

22 Handlebars

In 1817, the Draisine was fitted with the simplest kind of handlebar imaginable: a straight wooden bar that a rider would use for support and rudimentary steering. Since then, the purpose of a bicycle's handlebars – to enable a cyclist to control the direction of travel and generate power by applying greater pressure on the pedals – has not significantly changed. The design and technology, however, has.

The first modification came with the introduction of the Whatton bar, in the 1870s. Little is known of the inventor. This was used by riders of high-wheelers – who rested their thighs in a pair of metal loops, grasping the ends of the loops to steer – and enabled them to land on their feet in the event of an accident, thus (in theory) minimising their risk of 'taking a header'.

The earliest type of drop handlebar – which reduced air resistance and enabled riders to go faster – was developed in 1879, towards the end of the high-wheeler craze. However, this wasn't the only innovation taking place; in fact, so rapid was the development of different handlebar styles that, in 1880, *The Cyclist* magazine commented that: 'perhaps no single portion of the bicycle marks the general improvement of the age so much as the handle-bar.'

By the time the safety bicycle was developed in 1884, handlebars were offered in 'flat', 'upturned' or 'dropped' formulations. Straight handlebars were excellent for riding in a dignified and comfortable upright position, but if you wanted to go faster, exert more pressure on the pedal and minimise aerodynamic drag, then you needed to fold your body forwards over the bike. By making the middle of the bars the highest point and dropping the ends of the handlebars into a hook, the drop handlebar facilitates a lower, flatter position on the bike. The 'hooks' or 'drops' also offer a variety of different hand positions – an important consideration for modern professionals riding hundreds of kilometres a day.

One of the most enduring designs for drop handlebars is the 'Maes'. Named after Sylvère Maes, the Belgian rider who won the Tour de France in 1936 and 1939 and popularised the use of dropped handlebars in the peloton, the Maes is the classic completely curved drop handlebar that resembles a ram's horns. Anatomic bends, where a section of the lower part of the curve of the drops is flat, are also common.

Away from road racing, many other shapes and types of handlebar are used. True to their derivation from 1930s' and 1940s' leisure bikes, mountain bikes have straight handlebars that allow for a more upright riding position that enables the rider to brace and keep better control in tight turns and on rough ground. Most city and commuter bikes, such as the famous Dutch bike, use swept-back, upright handlebars known as North Road bars after London's North Road Cycling Club, where the style first emerged, probably in the 1890s.

Handlebars, like other bicycle components, are made from a range of materials. The Rover Safety Bicycle in the 1890s employed tubular steel, the use of which remains popular today, and the Italian bicycle manufacturer Cinelli is credited with introducing aluminium handlebars to the professional peloton in the 1960s. Carbon fibre, first used for handlebars by German Stefan Smolke in 1992, or alloy, are now the primary materials of choice.

Riding with the drop handlebars to which
he gave his name, Belgian Sylvère Maes
climbs the Col de l'Izoard during the 1936
Tour de France. Maes went on to win the
race in Paris, the first of his two victories.

23 Rim brake

The earliest bikes, the vélocipèdes of the 1860s and the 'ordinary' high-wheelers of the 1870s, were equipped with rudimentary rim brakes (so-called because of the interaction between the brake pads and the wheel rims). However, made of leather and wood, they suffered from excessive wear and tear, and were not particularly efficient.

In 1876 English inventors Browett and Harrison developed the first calliper-style rim brakes, a mechanism activated by a lever centrally mounted on the handlebars that pulled a cable attached to a pair of metal brake arms fitted with brake blocks either side of the wheel rim. When activated, the brake arms exerted a powerful pincer action, slowing the spinning wheel, an effect enhanced because the blocks were made of rubber, which provided superior friction when applied to metal. These are the ancestors of all modern rim brake systems that use friction to disperse the kinetic energy of the moving wheel.

The rise of the pneumatic-tyred safety bicycle during the boom of the 1890s further drove innovations in brake technology, and in America and Germany the coaster brake (see pp. 54–55) mounted in the hub of the rear wheel gained in popularity. In the UK, Raleigh first introduced roller lever brakes – also known as stirrup brakes – in 1910. This mechanism, which used a series of rods and pivots to pull felt pads onto the inside of the wheel rim, would become standard on Raleigh bikes from the 1930s.

Felt and cork pads remained popular during the 1920s and 1930s, particularly in America, where wooden wheel rims were the norm. There were also continuing doubts about rubber pads, that were estimated to lose 90 per cent of their efficiency in wet weather. But the introduction of the 'Dura' aluminium wheel rim in 1934 cemented rubber as the standard material for brake pads because of its enhanced grip in all conditions.

By the 1940s, the cable-operated, side-pull calliper brake had supplanted the more complex roller brake as the standard mechanism. Professional riders, however, wanted brakes that were more responsive. A great debate raged: side pulls or centre pulls? The evenness offered by the centre-pull system was a major advantage over the side-pull mechanism, which had a tendency for one brake pad to engage before the other. However, centre-pulls were robust and heavy and couldn't match the sleek, stylish lines and light weight of, for instance, the Campagnolo Record side-pull brake, which formed part of the first-ever groupset or gruppo (a completely integrated set of components manufactured by the same company) released in 1968. The Record also featured a quick-release mechanism-enable rapid in-race wheel changes. The sheer quality of the Record set the benchmark for side-pull brakes and it remains in production to this day.

For all their brilliance, however, the future for rim brakes may lie not with side- or centre-pull systems but with the science of hydraulics. Introduced when a patent was granted to Keizo Shimano and Yuji Fujii in 1969, the concept of a hydraulic rim brake that used a single lever to power the front and rear brakes sequentially has stuck around. In this early design, the brake calliper was powered by its own hydraulic piston and controlled by a two-piston master cylinder that ensured the brakes would not fail, even if a cylinder leaked. Subsequently, German company Magura did away with the callipers altogether, connecting the brake blocks directly to the pistons, allowing for an almost 100 per cent transfer of power between the brake lever and the brake block.

Since then, the latest innovation in braking technology has come not from the road but from mountain biking, in the form of the disc brake (see pp. 56-57).

A bicycle mechanic adjusts the front rim brake on a Brompton folding bicycle. Invented in 1876 by English inventors Browett and Harrison, the calliper-style rim brake remains popular for road bikes.

24 Coaster brake

The coaster brake is one of the three types of braking mechanism developed to slow down and stop a bike safely and efficiently. This mechanism quickly gained in popularity in the USA, Germany and the Netherlands in the 1890s and is still used for upright and children's bicycles.

The patent for the coaster brake – the first device to combine the functions of driving, coasting and braking – was granted in 1898 to Harry Pond Townsend of Connecticut, USA. He immediately assigned the manufacture of his new device to the New Departure Manufacturing Company. From then on its use became widespread in the USA, with the catalogue for Columbia cycles (on which it was used) proclaiming the coaster as being 'a device for which a need had long existed.' Townsend's New Departure automatic coaster brake was finally granted a patent in 1907.

Housed in the rear hub, the coaster or hub brake works by the rider pedalling backwards to activate a number of wedge-shaped blocks or discs that drag against the shell of the hub. The action of metal on metal generates friction that slows and then stops the rear wheel. Simple and effective, the technology of the coaster brake has barely changed since its invention. The coaster is also low-maintenance, as effective in the rain as in dry conditions, and requires no untidy cables between the handlebars and wheel, but these benefits are somewhat outweighed by the fact that the brakes may make it awkward to get a bike started, can fail catastrophically (rather than just gradually becoming less efficient), and have a tendency to overheat on a downhill, often causing bearing grease to liquefy, trailing a plume of smoke behind the bike.

In spite of these drawbacks, however, the brakes remained extremely popular and were used by cyclists all over the world, including Harry Green, who set a record for riding from Land's End to John O' Groats in 1908 – just one of several remarkable feats and long-distance cycling records. He had already set the mark for riding from London to Brighton and back two years previously.

Elsewhere, the Fichtel-Sachs Torpedo coaster brake was first developed in 1903 in Schweinfurt, Germany, and remained in production until 1991, one of the longest continuous production runs in cycling history. Manufacture only ceased when the Swiss Army, who had been the company's major customer for coaster brakes, switched from single-speed bikes to geared bikes fitted with derailleurs. The Torpedo operated via a roller clutch, using oversized roller bearings to jam against the hub instead of the wedges of the New Departure coaster brake. Sachs paid the New Departure company 3 million marks to licence their technology.

Other major manufacturers of the coaster included Sturmey-Archer, which had experimented with mounting a brake in their 3-speed gear hubs in 1918. In 1931, they licensed Perry & Co., one of the most important British producers of coaster brakes, and produced the K-series 3-Speed Hub, combining gearing and drum-braking capabilities. The difference between the drum brake and the coaster brake lay in the activation of the braking mechanism: instead of being triggered by back pedalling, the mechanical cam in the Sturmey-Archer K hub drum brake was linked to a brake lever with a Bowden cable.

As other brakes developed and single-speed bikes waned, coaster brakes became less widely used. Although they gained new-found popularity during the early days of mountain biking, they were superseded by calliper brakes in the 1970s (*see* pp. 52–53) and then disc brakes (*see* pp. 56–57), the modern reiteration of hub-gear technology.

The coaster brake was patented by Harry Pond Townsend, of New Britain, Connecticut on April 9, 1907. Reliable and easy to use, the coaster brake is popular in children's and touring bikes.

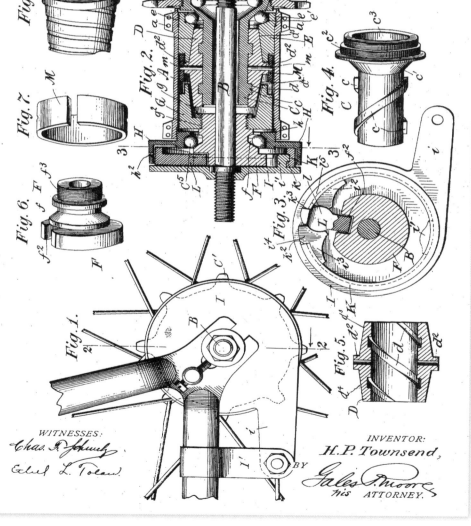

No. 850,077.

PATENTED APR. 9, 1907.

H. P. TOWNSEND.
DRIVING AND BRAKING MECHANISM FOR CYCLES.
APPLICATION FILED APR. 26, 1906.

WITNESSES:
Chas. F. Schmidt
Ethel L. Tolan.

INVENTOR:
H. P. Townsend,
BY Gales F. Moore
his ATTORNEY.

25 Disc brake

Disc brake technology is most commonly associated with the motorcar, but in fact disc brakes were first patented for the bicycle. In 1893, Joel Hendrick and Arthur Fay of Massachusetts, USA, applied for a patent for a disc brake featuring an aluminium rotor – the hub-mounted disc that, when pressed against the wheel, creates friction and stops the wheel spinning – with vulcanised rubber brake pads. These disc brakes were not a success and they more or less disappeared.

Until, that is, 1971, when Shimano applied for a disc brake patent and began to market their product. By 1975 they were offering cable-actuated and hydraulic disc brakes, promising 'no slippage, even in rain'. Despite this, disc brakes were perceived as being difficult to fit and adjust, and parts were in short supply, and it languished on the periphery of the brake-technology scene.

This disc brake uses a calliper attached to the frame to apply pressure to the spinning disc (or rotor) attached to the hub, producing friction and stopping the wheel. It can be argued that it is simply an adaptation of the rim brake – and the application of force to create friction and stopping power is essentially the same – but there are several distinct advantages to disc braking. First, it generates a great deal of power; second, force can be applied more evenly and reliably and with a lighter touch; and third, the disc rotor is far more efficient at displacing water and the braking surface is further away from mud and moisture, making disc brakes much more effective than rim brakes in poor weather. Disc brakes are also perforated, which allows heat from friction build-up to dissipate, and they can be activated by a standard brake cable or by hydraulic pistons. Moving the braking surface away from the wheel rim also prolongs wheel lifetimes.

For mountain biking, there was one other huge benefit to this new braking technology. As a wheel's rim becomes damaged and no longer runs true, rim brakes start to rub against it and lose their effectiveness. This problem doesn't occur with the hub-mounted rotor, which continues to be effective whatever the weather and whatever the damage to the wheel rim.

In 2016, the UCI decided to trial disc-brake technology on professional road bikes. Although a disc brake gives riders far greater braking power, allowing them to brake later into a corner and to carry more speed coming out of it, there are distinct disadvantages for road-race use. Disc brakes are much heavier than featherlight rim brakes. There are also concerns about how much impact the hub-mounted disc brake will have on the fast wheel changes necessary for a professional race. Speaking to *Cycling Tips* in 2016, Philip Gilbert raised concerns about riders coming into contact with a hot spinning rotor disc during a crash. Gilbert's concerns seemed to be legitimised when Fran Ventoso of Movistar suffered a terrible leg injury at Paris–Roubaix that year, claiming it was as a result of coming into contact with a rotor disc (although subsequent investigation found a bicycle chain was a more probable cause). The UCI swiftly suspended the trial. However, disc-braking technology was approved for amateur mass-ride events such as gran fondos and sportives, although they remain banned in Federation Française Cyclisme events like the Etape du Tour.

It remains to be seen whether the peloton will embrace the disc brake. After all, there are very different race conditions to those found in mountain biking and cyclocross, branches of the sport in which disc brakes have been enthusiastically embraced. For amateur riders, however, the disc brake's combination of power, reliability and performance makes this the braking technology of the future.

Though originally patented by Joel Hendrick and Arthur Fay in 1893, the disk brake is only now breaking through into the professional peloton. Renowned for its superior braking performance in wet weather conditions, it is popular in mountain and cyclocross bikes.

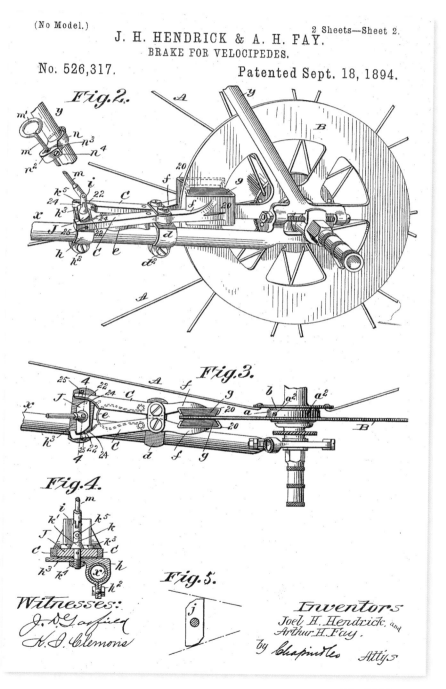

(No Model.)

2 Sheets—Sheet 2.

J. H. HENDRICK & A. H. FAY.
BRAKE FOR VELOCIPEDES.

No. 526,317.

Patented Sept. 18, 1894.

Fig.2.

Fig.3.

Fig.4.

Fig.5.

Witnesses:

Inventors
Joel H. Hendrick, and
Arthur H. Fay.
by Chapin &co Attys

26 Cycling cap/*casquette*

Professional cycling has long been considered a route to social mobility in Europe. Take as an example the 1925 Tour de France. On the start line in Paris were five mechanics, four farmers, three builders (including the Italian winner, Ottavio Bottecchia), two miners, two butchers and two locksmiths. Not surprisingly, the press dubbed the race the 'Tour des Artisans'. For many racers the sport was a way out of the back-breaking toil of mining or agricultural labour and a route to celebrity and riches – one that their fitness, thanks to a life of sheer hard graft, had left them well equipped to pursue.

And it was thanks to those artisans in the early part of the 20th century, who were used to finding practical solutions to working outdoors and in testing conditions, that the cycling cap or *casquette* found its way into the peloton. Images of early races show riders in berets, flat caps or brimless skullcaps – everyday headgear that served the purpose of keeping the sun and the rain off a rider's face. Riders in vélocipède races adopted the jockey's cap, which was close-fitting enough to remain in place even at speed, while soldiers in the bicycle regiments of World War I adopted a type of khaki cap or *casquette* as part of their uniform.

This last type of headwear has had enduring appeal, as Colin Lewis, a member of the 1967 Great Britain team at the Tour de France, explained to *Bicycling* magazine in 2014: 'No one had helmets, and a cap was very practical; firstly it would keep the sun out of our eyes, secondly it absorbed the sweat, and thirdly it kept the rain and muck

out.' A cycling cap is also a handy billboard for the sponsor, and began to have greater value in the 1970s when production costs fell and thousands were produced to hand out at races to the watching crowds.

Worn backwards or forwards, high on the crown of the head or pulled low over the brow, peak down or turned up, the cycling cap enjoyed its heyday during the period from the 1960s to the end of the 1980s, when it was worn by professionals as the insignia of their trade and by amateurs in emulation of their idols. However, in 1991, the UCI made helmets mandatory for amateurs and, in 2003, sounded the death knell for the *casquette* when helmets became compulsory for professionals too. For a new generation of professional riders, many from outside the European tradition, the baseball hat has now become the podium-wear of choice.

Despite this, the cap refuses to disappear and is often seen poking from beneath the helmets of professional and amateur riders, especially in wet conditions. Its appeal has crossed over to the fixie riders (a 'fixie' is a bike without a freewheel and often no brakes that has many supporters), and hipsters. Its perfect blend of form and functionality have won fans such as Mark Cavendish, who insists on wearing a cap and has designed his own, and there is even a movement called 'Caps not Hats', which has its own #capsnothats hashtag. As American cycling writer Bill Strickland puts it: 'One thing I love about cycling is the odd traditions that still exist no matter how hi-tech it gets. The cycling cap is one of these.' *Chapeau!*

Eddy Merckx sports one of the most iconic *casquettes* in cycling, compete with Molteni sponsorship, at the 1971 Tour de France. These lightweight cloth caps were both functional and stylish.

Helmet

The modern cycling helmet is usually composed of a foam liner encased in a plastic shell with a simple strap and snap fastening. They are lightweight, compact and – if fitted correctly – offer a high degree of impact protection. The use of helmets in professional cycling has been mandatory since 2003, following the death of Andreï Kivilev from Kazakhstan during the Paris–Nice race. But the laws are different for recreational riders. For example, in France, Germany, the Netherlands and the UK there is no requirement to wear a helmet whereas their use is mandatory in Australia.

The earliest form of helmet was the pith helmet – also known as the sola topee or sun helmet – and was widely used by Europeans in India and the tropics during the days of Empire to provide sun protection. Made of pith, a crushable cork-like material, they provided single-impact protection for 'ordinary' riders who had 'taken a header'.

Next came a kind of leather skullcap or hairnet, consisting of strips of cowhide bound together with a wool-padded leather rim. Later versions – as popularised by French rider Jean Robic in the 1940s and 1950s, who was nicknamed 'tête de cuir' or 'leather head' as a result – consisted of foam padding bound in leather, but their protection level was minimal and they were prone to rotting over time. Despite this, the 'hairnet' remained in use in the professional sport until the 1970s.

In fact, the bicycle helmet might not have evolved further had it not been for two major developments: the increasing number of cars on the roads, and the rise in popularity of the bicycle. While the professional peloton switched to using the cloth casquette, the race was on to find a reliable method of protecting everyday cyclists from potentially fatal head injuries. In the 1970s, when the Snell Institute in America ran comprehensive safety tests on the helmets available, only a light motorbike helmet passed, which was hot, heavy and uncomfortable to wear.

It wasn't until 1975 that the Californian firm Bell Helmets – founded by Roy Richter in 1954 to manufacture hard-shell protective headgear for racing drivers – invented the first modern cycling helmet. By encasing a foam liner in a lightweight hard plastic shell, they developed the blueprint for the kind of helmets in use today. The real innovation was to replace squashy foam liners with rigid expanded polystyrene, which provided hugely improved protection against all-over impact.

In the UK alone, around 21,000 people were reported injured as a result of cycling accidents in 2014, more than 3500 of them killed or seriously injured. Some of these deaths may have been avoidable: the simple act of wearing a helmet is estimated to reduce the risk of head injury by 85 per cent, yet in the UK only 14 per cent of riders wear a helmet regularly. In Australia, where helmet use is compulsory, deaths fell by 45 per cent the year after the legislation was introduced in 1990.

The subject of compulsory helmet wearing is, however, a controversial one, with cycling advocates claiming that driver education is more important than protection. This was somewhat undermined by a study in 2015 by University College Dublin, which concluded that deaths can be prevented by the 'significant protection' that a helmet offers.

Though the outer shell varies in style, and the liner may now be made of a variety of other rigid foams or even corrugated cardboard, the standard helmet design has changed little since the 1970s. New designs and innovations underway, however, are becoming more futuristic, with inflatable air bags to protect the head in the event of a collision already available on the market.

Jean Robic, wearing the leather skullcap that earned him the nickname 'leather head', shown during a stage of the 1953 Tour de France.

Goggles/sunglasses

Before Aviators and Eyeshades and Jawbones, there were the humble goggles sported either high on the forehead, covering the eyes or, for fashion purposes, slung casually around the forearm in the style preferred by Switzerland's Hugo Koblet, the winner of the 1951 Tour de France, a rider known for his sense of style.

Developed around the turn of the 20th century, goggles were worn by such early cycling stars as French rider Octave Lapize, Belgian Philipe Thys and Italian Ottavio Bottecchia. Similar to the kind of heavy leather goggles Lapize would later wear as a pilot during World War I, these leather-and-glass goggles were invaluable during the early races, which took place on roads that were often unpaved and were sometimes little more than cart tracks through the mountains. Eye injuries caused by flicked-up road debris could be severe. Honoré Barthélémy, for instance, lost an eye after he was struck by a piece of flint (he hadn't noticed there was a problem during the race, since he was already in such terrible pain from other injuries he'd received as he crashed repeatedly), and rode for the rest of his career with a glass eye that often fell out – the Frenchman would claim he'd spent more on glass eyes than he'd earned in prize money.

Modified flying goggles – now with rubber replacing the heavy leather strapping – remained the eyewear of choice in the peloton until the 1950s, when Fausto Coppi began sporting Ray-Ban Aviators that were popular with film stars and celebrities of the day. These and similar sunglasses became the eyewear of choice for many in the peloton, and off it, for the next 35 years or so. Until, that is, an American wearing frames designed by a motorbike components' manufacturer blazed the trail that cycling stars still follow today.

Jim Jannard had started his career developing motorcycle grips before moving on to invent the Oakley brand and designing the Oakley O-Frame motorbike and skiing goggles. In 1984, champion road-racing cyclist Greg LeMond approached Jannard for a pair of eyeshades, debuting them on the peloton. With their exaggerated ski-goggle-style shape, huge lenses and bright colours, Oakley Eyeshades quickly became iconic, especially when LeMond went on to become the first American to win the Tour de France in 1986.

While Aviators and later Oakleys became popular in the peloton, other short- or long-sighted riders simply opted for standard glasses. These included Laurent Fignon, nicknamed 'the Professor' because of his round John Lennon-style frames, and Dutchman Jan Janssen, who sported prescription sunglasses. In the 1990s Oakley integrated prescription lenses into their frames, including those of Swiss rider Alex Zülle, whose extremely poor eyesight impacted on his descending skills.

Road conditions have improved hugely since Barthélémy's day, but sunglasses still play a valuable role in protecting a rider's eyes from rain, dust and flying objects. Polycarbonate lenses have become a popular alternative to glass, proving virtually unbreakable and mist-free in damp conditions. More importantly, sunglasses guard against the risk of cataracts and UV damage caused by long exposure to sunlight. Wraparound, anti-glare styles are doubly effective, providing both essential sun protection and superior peripheral vision, allowing riders to safely navigate their way around a speeding peloton. Frames can also now be customised to match leaders' jerseys, from yellow to polka dot, and inbuilt technologies to provide heads-up displays, similar to Google Glass, are already being tested in the peloton.

Italian *Campionissimo* Fausto Coppi
sporting his iconic Ray-Ban Aviators as
he's congratulated after winning the
1949 Tour de France. It was the first of
his two wins in the French Grand Tour.

Jersey

Photos from the 1870s reveal that the pioneering 'ordinary' racers wore adaptations of their everyday clothing manufactured from the fabrics of the day, such as cotton short-sleeved vests, tweed knickerbockers and woollen jerseys. Wool may seem like a surprising fabric for a jersey, but in fact it is an excellent choice because, thanks to its texture, it is surprisingly efficient at wicking moisture away from the skin. It also has a degree of stretch, is comfortable to wear and absorbs perspiration well.

There was one major problem, however, with fashioning jerseys out of wool for use in sport: the elements. Wool jerseys grew heavy, baggy and shapeless in the rain (often smelling like the sheep they came from), and didn't allow enough airflow on a tough mountain climb. An alternative was needed, and it was an Italian tailor who made the breakthrough. Armando Castelli, who had been working for small clothing company, Vittore Gianni in Milan during the 1940s, was approached by Fausto Coppi to create a lighter and cooler jersey. In response, Castelli hit on the idea of using silk.

By the 1950s, the silk jersey had made inroads into the peloton. Two years later Gino Bartali and Coppi both wore Castelli silk jerseys as they battled for supremacy in the 1952 Tour. Some riders clung to the old ways, including Louison Bobet, the French champion of the 1950s, who would never wear anything but wool, claiming it was more hygienic (Bobet suffered terribly with a skin condition).

One huge advantage of silk – at least for sponsors – was that it took ink extremely well, a highly desirable feature since having your company's name emblazoned on a rider's chest was of paramount importance for effective advertising. The introduction of silk and new sublimation dye processes heralded the beginning of the kaleidoscopic peloton we see today. For its originator, the use of silk lent itself to new design touches, and Castelli soon began crafting jerseys with zips, pockets and collars.

In 1941, J.T. Dickson and Rex Whinfield patented PET or polyester, paving the way for the man-made fabrics that were to follow. These new fabrics, particularly Lycra, had the lightness and feel of silk, could be combined with other fabrics to preserve the wicking qualities of wool but were, crucially, skin-tight and aerodynamic, offering designers the opportunity to put into practice new research on ways that riders could reduce wind drag.

In 1974, Armando Castelli's son Maurizio relaunched the brand with a signature scorpion logo. Maurizio had grown up in the sports clothing business and was passionate and innovative. As an ex-rider, he had a clear understanding of the high-performance clothing a professional cyclist required. The brand quickly became synonymous with quality and was worn by the most famous riders of the day, including Eddy Merckx. Castelli clothing dominated the cycling apparel industry until Maurizio's early death in 1995, which occurred while the innovative designer was riding his bike up the famous Cipressa climb in San Remo, Italy.

The latest innovation in cycling jerseys is the mesh jersey (or 'climber's jersey' as it is sometimes known). They are super-light and extremely breathable, thanks to their mesh-panel design. Always at the forefront of new cycling technology, Team Sky trialled a mesh skinsuit in 2014, though the combination of mesh and a Lycra 'modesty' pouch was felt to be a step too far. According to Chris Froome, however, it took 'marginal gains to the next level', though he suffered severe sunburn when wearing it.

Great rivals Fausto Coppi in the iconic Bianchi jersey, and Gino Bartali riding for his own Bartali team, competing in 1952. Both are wearing silk jerseys that were cooler and lighter than wool, and took ink extremely well, making them the forerunner of today's kaleidoscopic peloton.

30 Lycra

When Joseph C. Shivers, armed with a doctorate in chemistry, arrived at the DuPont research laboratory in 1949, he had no idea he was about to revolutionise the face of fashion and sportswear.

Chemists at DuPont had already discovered Nylon in 1938, but the search was on to produce a synthetic, patentable alternative to rubber for use in clothing, and in particular ladies' underwear. Following an early experiment in the late 1940s that had failed to produce a material with the necessary 'snap-back'-ability required for women's corsetry, the project was shelved. Until, that is, Shivers conducted a series of experiments in the 1950s that stabilised the elastomer molecules and allowed them to rebound. Thus was born Dacron, which, after refinement, became in 1959 the new polyester, called spandex or elastane. Initially named Fibre K by DuPont, spandex – an anagram of 'expands' – was later called Lycra (a brand of spandex manufactured by the Invista company), though the terms elastane, spandex and Lycra are commonly used these days.

Lycra/spandex is a long-chain synthetic polymeric fibre in which soft and rubbery polyester allows for stretch while harder urethanes provide rigidity. According to Shivers: 'the polymer started out like water, but then thickened up after an hour or two. It produced a very viscous substance.' This substance could stretch to 500 times its original length, be spun into fine filaments and, most importantly, snap back into shape time after time after time. In 1962, Lycra went on sale to the general public and was initially used in hosiery and underwear, but it quickly revolutionised sportswear and was worn at the 1968 Grenoble Winter Games by the French Olympic ski team. By 1972, Olympic swimmers were wearing sleek contoured suits in the new wonder fabric and gymnasts too were soon tumbling and twirling in Lycra leotards. From thereon in, spandex had hit the mainstream, no doubt helped along by the fitness boom of the 1980s – think Olivia Newton-John getting physical and Jane Fonda going for the burn.

As for cycling, Lycra proved itself an ideal material for the endurance athlete. First, it is supremely comfortable, ensuring that clothing retains its shape and doesn't sag or bag, however hard a rider pounds the pedals. It also dries quickly, an advantage after a long commute or a Tour de France stage, and its form-fitting qualities lessen aerodynamic drag, allowing a cyclist to go faster with less effort. Finally, Lycra's ability to absorb ink means it can carry any colour or design – a boon for sponsors and the more flamboyant members of the peloton, such as Italian cyclist Mario Cipollini, who was famed for his creative skinsuits ranging from animal prints to a 'muscle suit' resembling human anatomy.

Lycra revolutionised sportswear, being comfortable, moisture-wicking and extremely aerodynamic. The flamboyant Italian sprinter Mario Cipollini, seen here in his infamous 'muscle' suit, fully exploited the qualities of Lycra in a range of outrageous skinsuits.

Cycling shorts

As with many other items of cycling gear, cycling shorts developed organically from everyday garments in the early days of the sport, when there were no technical fibres such as Lycra to make long days in the saddle more comfortable.

Wool was the first material of choice for cyclists, but woollen shorts quickly became baggy and would bunch uncomfortably. In the 1930s, therefore, designers began to experiment with multi-panelled shorts to overcome the problems of poor fit, but with panels came seams that caused friction and painful saddle sores. The solution? A padded insert made from the hide of the Chamois.

Chamois, a type of goat-antelope native to the Alps, Pyrenees and Caucasus Mountains, yields a hide that is gentle, absorbent and non-abrasive, but that is prone to drying and cracking after repeated use. Modern chamois substitutes are generally now made of moisture-wicking polyester fabrics and remain supple and absorbent. However, even with modern substitutes, chamois cream – traditionally used to restore condition to authentic chamois hide – is useful for creating an anti-friction barrier between the skin and the pad, as well as promoting an antiseptic and anti-fungal environment.

Another innovation to improve the function and comfort of shorts was the use of braces to keep them securely in place. Primitive versions of these 'bib shorts' as they are called first appeared in a photograph of Eddy Merckx in the late 1960s, and simply consisted of normal woollen shorts attached to standard braces for trousers.

A few years later came the next major step forwards: Lycra shorts, for which both the Swiss company Assos and the Italian firm Castelli claim credit. Assos claimed these were developed almost by accident in the mid-1970s when Toni Maier-Moussa, former Swiss pro rider, owner of Assos and cycling innovator, discovered that a rider wearing a Lycra skiing suit performed better in wind-tunnel tests than they did with naked skin. Maier-Moussa promptly clad the team he sponsored in his cycling-specific Lycra shorts, and these proved so beneficial in terms of comfort and improved aerodynamics that despite costing up to three times more than standard woollen shorts, big names started to buy them, starting with Peter Post and his TI-Raleigh team in 1977. Castelli, however, assert that they were first to the market in 1977 with Lycra shorts for use by professionals and the public.

Whoever really did start the trend for Lycra shorts, it was the Italian company Santini that created the first black Lycra bib shorts in 1979. The advantages were obvious: well-fitting bib shorts stayed put, avoiding the potential for embarrassing exposure, and supported the core muscles during vigorous exertion. They also held the chamois securely in place. By the 1980s, bib shorts had become standard attire for the professional peloton and they are still widely used – although some riders claim they are uncomfortably restrictive and make bathroom breaks considerably more difficult.

In 1981, the world of cycling was rocked by the arrival at the Giro of a group of riders who, having stripped off their black wool leggings, revealed turquoise shorts underneath – the first coloured shorts ever worn. Behind the stunt was Castelli, who was heavily fined, since at that time only black shorts were permitted, but the media frenzy and day-long coverage of the innovation meant the penalty was worth every penny.

Since then, restrictions on the colour of shorts have been lifted, and Lycra of every hue imaginable clads the thighs of cyclists the world over, though the chamois has remained pretty much the same.

Lycra cycling shorts have been around since the mid-1970s. At the 1981 Giro d'Italia, Castelli outfitted a handful of riders with turquoise Lycra shorts – at a time when only black shorts were allowed. A media frenzy followed, including day-long television coverage of the turquoise lycra shorts.

32 Razor

It is one of the most frequently asked questions in cycling: why do professional cyclists shave their legs?

Although nobody really knows why or how or when it started, it is believed that even the early professional cyclists did it and it is now the norm, as American rider Davis Phinney, who raced in the 1980s, explained: 'It was the fashion when I raced. It's the fashion now. Real bike riders shave their legs.'

The most frequently cited reasons for cyclists having hairless legs are: health – road rash heals more quickly and cleanly; comfort – a massage is considerably more enjoyable and effective when your leg hair isn't being tugged continually; and science – shaving helps the pursuit of aerodynamic gains, as outlined in a study conducted in 1987 by Chester Kyle for *Bicycling* magazine.

Kyle's claims were certainly persuasive and his conclusion that the aerodynamic improvement offered by leg shaving being roughly five seconds in a 40km (25-mile) time-trial ridden at 37kph (23mph), became a mantra for cyclists. Any marginal gain is worth exploiting, but the effect was thought to be largely psychological – the more aerodynamic you look and feel, the more aerodynamic you will be. Davis Phinney again: 'I know that if I ever looked down while I was on the bike and saw hairy legs I immediately felt slower.'

In 2014, American triathlete Jesse Thomas had neglected to shave before a series of tests in the Specialized bike factory's wind tunnel. The results were astonishing. A human Chewbacca, Thomas is naturally hirsute. Once shorn of his leg hair, however, his drag was reduced by 7 per cent, the equivalent to a whopping 79 seconds in a 40km (25-mile) time-trial. Mark Cote and Chris Yu, both Specialized employees who are experts in aerodynamics, repeated the testing with five other equally hairy cyclists and found the results to be consistent, with savings of between 50 and 82 seconds over the distance.

So how could the Kyle data be so out of kilter with Cote and Yu's findings? Well, it turns out that Kyle had used a miniature wind tunnel and a fake leg with hair glued to it to achieve his results, so little wonder that they were so at odds with tests with real humans. Cote and Yu are now testing the efficacy of arm shaving.

And what about technique? Briton Sean Yates, one of the hard men of cycling and one-time staff member at Team Sky, told the Australian *Cycling Tips* website in 2011 that the best way to shave is in a bath, with a ladies' razor. The image of the strapping ex-professional with a pink razor in his hand is a bizarre one – but as Cote and Yu's research has proved, this is one marginal gain that any rider can make use of.

A general view of athletes' legs the Elite Men's Road Race, in Italy in 2013. In wind tunnel testing in 2014, leg shaving was proved definitively to be more aerodynamic.

33 Energy gel

Although the sight of riders in the peloton sucking down energy gels from foil packets is now a common one, the first energy gel wasn't invented until 1986. Before then, the contents of a cyclist's musette (bag) had more to do with quick energy fixes and some strange dietary practices based on hearsay and folklore rather than sound nutritional advice.

In the earliest days of the sport, it wasn't uncommon to see riders raiding a local café for anything they could scavenge, including beer, wine and baguettes. But modern sports science has researched and refined the nutritional requirements an endurance athlete needs – water and energy. Energy gels provide concentrated sugars for a quick and easily absorbed energy hit.

The first studies of carbohydrate and fat metabolism were conducted in Sweden in the 1930s. Thirty-five years later, in 1965, Dr Robert Cade invented a scientifically formulated recovery drink for his University of Florida football team and called it Gatorade after the team mascot. He never looked back, and the sports drink industry is now worth in excess of £4 billion (US$5 billion) annually. However, despite the flooding of the market with these sugary drinks in the 1960s and 1970s, the actual science of sports nutrition didn't really take off until the 1980s, when the impact of nutrition on training and recovery became better understood.

Exercise physiologists were also discovering the kind of carbohydrate load that endurance athletes needed for maximum performance. In response to their discoveries, sports nutritionists began the search for alternative energy-delivery systems to the sports drinks, and the first energy bars came on to the market in the mid-1980s. These were far from perfect, however, since although they

avoided the internal distress that could be caused by consuming large quantities of sports drink, the new energy bars were often chewy and difficult to digest.

The energy gel overcame these issues, delivering easily and quickly metabolised energy to replace depleted muscle glycogen stores, all wrapped in a handily portable package (although riders in long-distance events often start out eating solid food, such as small sandwiches, energy bars, rice cakes and even cake, before switching to energy gels later on). A typical energy gel will contain carbohydrates, electrolytes to replace those lost through sweating, and sometimes a stimulant such as caffeine. They are particularly effective at warding off hypoglaecemia – the dreaded 'bonk' that is the cyclists' equivalent of hitting the marathon runner's 'wall'.

The timing of snacks is extremely important for several reasons, not least because there are rules about how many and when the gels can be used during a professional race: UCI rule 2.3.027 states that taking food from a teammate is prohibited during the last 10km of a climb or within the last 20km on flat stages. Sometimes, however, riders are forced to go against the regulations and take some food in order to stave off the bonk, as was the case for Britain's Chris Froome in the 2013 Tour de France. Despite having been given a 20-second penalty for consuming an energy gel within the last 20km of the Alpe d'Huez stage, he still went on to win the Tour.

Energy gels, then, play an important role in sustaining pro athletes – who during the Tour de France, for example, need to consume a whopping 5000–8000 calories per day, along with up to 10 litres of water – but are equally useful for recreational bikers due to their portability, ease of use while on the move, and effectiveness.

Belgian cycling star Tom Boonen takes an energy gel while out training in 2015. Energy gels are portable, easy to use and effective for pros and recreational riders alike.

34 Newspaper

Newspaper – or rather one French sports paper – has played an absolutely crucial role in the development of cycling. The fact is, without *L'Auto*, the Tour de France and the subsequent evolution of the sport of bicycle stage racing would simply never have occurred.

The story begins in the early 20th century when, seeking a way of promoting his fledgling newspaper, editor-in-chief Henri Desgrange sat down for lunch with his second-in-command, Géo Lefèvre, to discuss ways that *L'Auto* might make its mark. Lefèvre, an accomplished amateur cyclist who had already toyed with the idea of a bicycle race to connect all the major French cities, put this notion to Desgrange, who agreed this was an excellent idea (for which he mostly went on to take the credit).

Announced on 19 January, 1903, the first Tour de France was ... a flop. Nobody was interested in riding a six-week race around the back roads of France nor the expense doing so would incur. Lefèvre and Desgrange went back to the drawing board, halving the duration of the race to three weeks. Seventy-eight riders duly signed up, and history was made.

The Giro d'Italia followed in 1909, sponsored by the *Gazzetta dello Sport* in a bid to attract readers away from the *Corriere della Serai*, a rival paper that was planning a tour of Italy of its own. Like the Tour, the Giro continues to present a leader's jersey that reflects the colour of the paper it was once printed on – yellow for *L'Auto* and pink for the *Gazzetta*.

The idea of using a bicycle race to promote a newspaper quickly gained traction. One-day classics including the Tour of Lombardy (1905), Tour of Flanders (1913), La Flèche Wallonne (1936) and Omloop Het Volk (1945) were all the creation of enterprising journalists. In addition, the traditional Tour de France warm-up, the Critérium du Dauphiné, was created by the local *Le Dauphiné Libéré* newspaper in 1947 to boost flagging post-war circulation.

The reason that these events were so successful was that there exists a perfect synergy between the drama of a cycling race and the need for compelling newspaper content – and so the sport and the press flourished.

Desgrange, meanwhile, continued to evolve the Tour, taking it to the high passes of the Alps and Pyrenees in 1910 and 1911. There, cyclists found they quickly needed a solution to an unforeseen problem – how to keep warm as they plunged down descents from the chilly heights to the warmer valley below. The answer: stuffing your jersey with material that's cheap, light and abundantly available to provide a useful windbreak for the chest and to warm and insulate the core. Yes, that's right, newspaper, and in particular the one that was full of the news of the race in question, *L'Auto*. Clever thinking.

With a nod to tradition and despite the fact that modern cycling gear is designed and engineered to wick moisture from the skin and trap and hold heat in its fibres, soigneurs (cyclists' carers) and spectators still hand out sheets of newspaper to the peloton as they swoop down the descents of the Alps or the Dolomites, which some riders stuff up their jerseys to create an extra barrier against windchill. Why do they still do it? Because it works. There are some traditions, it seems, that modern technology cannot replace.

An edition of *L'Auto Velo*, published on 15th May, 1897. Without French newspaper *L'Auto* and its editor, the autocratic Henri Desgrange, the sport of bicycle stage racing would not exist.

Marginal Gains

35 Aero time-trial bars

One of the most significant developments in cycling aerodynamics, aero time-trial bars didn't originate in the rarefied atmosphere of the great European stage races, but in one of the most gruelling endurance events of them all – the Race Across America (RAAM).

In fact, the story of the 'cowhorn' bars starts in a wind tunnel in Switzerland – the same wind tunnel where Toni Maier-Moussa, the Swiss engineer, ex-professional cyclist and innovator also developed the Lycra skinsuit. In 1976, Maier-Moussa was in the process of testing the world's first carbon-fibre bike, also designed and built by him, when he discovered that a rider's position was critical to their aerodynamic efficiency. By lowering and flipping the bars, so they pointed downwards rather than up, a cyclist was forced into a more streamlined position and tests in the wind tunnel revealed that this made a big difference. Little wonder, then, that cowhorn bars quickly became the time-trialling equipment of choice for the 1980s peloton.

Back to the 1984 RAAM, a gruelling combination of endurance stage race and off-road adventure that takes international riders from the West to the East Coast of the USA. At 1.93m (6ft 4in), Jim Elliott was huge for a racer. Despite this, earlier that year he had set a new 24-hour velodrome record, but this was his first shot at racing on the open road. Elliot's major problem was minimising wind drag on his large torso and it was his trainer, Richard Byrne – who would go on to invent the Speedplay pedal (*see* pp. 46–47) – who came up with the solution.

Byrne equipped Elliott's bike with what was referred to at the time as a 'lay down apparatus', which was, to all intents and purposes, the first set of aero bars. These consisted of a pair of carbon-fibre arm rests that projected back from the bars and hinged like a pair of sunglasses so they could be folded away when not in use in the climbs. On the flat, these armrests were very effective, and enabled Elliott to comfortably adopt a flat-backed posture and more efficiently cut through the air.

However, the aero bars that gained traction in the fledgling sport of triathlon were designed by a ski coach and manufactured by a US ski company, SCOTT. In 1989, the first prototypes, made of wood and intended to mimic the crouch position of a downhill skier, were tested downhill in Sun Valley, Idaho, where it quickly became clear that riders using the bars, even without pedalling, descended more quickly by some considerable margin. SCOTT donated bars to competitors in the new sport and they were soon a must-have item.

Cycling was slow to see the benefits of the new technology, preferring the old cowhorn bars, until the aero bars' superiority was crushingly demonstrated by Greg LeMond in the final stage of the 1989 Tour de France. Frenchman Laurent Fignon was only 50 seconds ahead of the American, but with just a 25km (15 ½ mile) time-trial between him and glory, Fignon chose to ride bareheaded with cowhorn bars. LeMond, by contrast, used an aerodynamic helmet and SCOTT aero bars and subsequently beat Fignon in that final time-trial, winning the race by eight seconds – the smallest winning margin ever in the Tour de France. The aero bar had made history, and has never looked back since.

American champion Greg LeMond shown riding
past the Champs-Elysees during the last stage of
the 1989 Tour de France. LeMond used Aero TT
bars to beat Laurent Fignon by eight seconds,
the smallest winning margin in history.

36 Time-trial helmet

The unique teardrop shape of the modern time-trial helmet has been developed to solve one of the major issues that face all professional racing cyclists: how to increase aerodynamic efficiency.

When riding in a peloton, cyclists benefit from the ability to draft or slipstream behind their fellow riders and thus reduce drag. In a time-trial, when a rider is alone on the road or track against the clock, they are unable to utilise this drafting effect and have to use far more energy to overcome their resistance to the air and achieve their maximum sustainable speed.

When Bernard Hinault won the prologue of the 1985 Tour de France – a race he went on to win for a record-equalling fifth time – he did so wearing a Cinelli Aerolite, a helmet with a distinctive teardrop shape. Built specifically to be as aerodynamic as possible, the Aerolite had neither vents nor any kind of protective padding. The Limar F104 followed in 1993, when it was the lightest aerodynamic helmet in production and boasted 10 vents to complement its tapered tail.

However, it was an American who would push the frontiers of time-trialling technology. In 1989, when Greg LeMond beat Laurent Fignon by 58 seconds in the climactic time-trial and won the Tour de France by eight seconds – he did so wearing a Giro Aerohead helmet. Having debuted a longtail version of the same helmet in the prologue, only to see it promptly banned, he wore the shorter version for the stage-five time-trial that he went on to win. Moreover, when he battled against Fignon for the overall title on the Champs-Elysées – when Fignon chose to ride bareheaded – the groundbreaking helmet was part of the aerodynamic armoury that saw LeMond become the first American to win the Tour.

Borrowing from the design of a children's safety helmet and lacking a hard exterior shell, the all-EPS (expanded polystyrene) helmet spawned a host of imitators, such as the Specialized Sub 6, which weighed a mere 170g (6oz). In 1999, inspired by John Cobb, the aerodynamics expert who was working with a young Texan rider, Giro produced the Rev V – a helmet designed to be aerodynamic even when a rider's posture caused it to tilt upwards – which Lance Armstrong used to win every individual test against the clock at the 1999 Tour. However, until the UCI introduced compulsory helmet-wearing ruling in 2003, these helmets offered no protection and were effectively simple aerodynamic fairings (or simple structures) fitted around the head.

The time-trial helmet has continued to evolve through innovations such as dual-foam technology (whereby the side sections were made from high-density foam and the centre and top parts from low-density foam); the ability to switch the aero mode on and off during a race by opening or closing vents using a slider button on the top of the helmet; and lower-drag, higher-cooling systems that combined optimal rider comfort with aerodynamic efficiency.

The aerodynamic benefits of the time-trial helmet have also crossed over to road racing helmet design. For the 2011 World Championships, Britain's Mark Cavendish used a helmet with the vents taped shut for improved aerodynamic efficiency. Noticing the benefits for flat races and those in cooler conditions, Giro then produced the Air Attack. In 2014, the Sky team wore the Kask Protone helmet, which featured wide, open-frontal vents (rather than the more standard closed-vent bowling-ball shape of other aero helmets) and was designed to provide adjustable aerodynamic performance according to several variables, including where a rider positioned his sunglasses.

Bernard Hinault rides at the 1985 Tour de France, wearing a Cinelli Aerolite helmet. The distinctive teardrop shape was designed specifically to be as aerodynamic as possible.

③⁷ Skinsuit

From Peter Post's all-conquering TI-Raleigh team to Mario Cipollini's muscle suit to Team Sky's philosophy of marginal gains, skinsuits are the ultimate go-faster wear for the modern cyclist.

Team Sky has become synonymous with the phrase 'marginal gains'; the philosophy of accumulating small time gains by looking at every aspect of a cyclist's performance – from the clothing he wears to the pillow he sleeps on – and some say this is the reason behind Team Sky's success. There is no more visible symbol of marginal gains than the skinsuits that Bradley Wiggins and Chris Froome wore to victory in the biggest race of them all, the Tour de France.

However, the story of the skinsuit begins in 1976, in the wind tunnel where Toni Maier-Moussa was testing his prototype carbon-fibre bike. He discovered that however light and aerodynamic the bike, it was the surface area of the rider that was the biggest contributing factor to aerodynamic drag. During the course of further tests he discovered that Lycra was more aerodynamically efficient than naked skin, and thus was born Lycra shorts (*see* pp. 68–69). More tests, undertaken at the Zurich Technical University in 1978, revealed that the gap between shorts and jersey also created a lot of drag, so Maier-Moussa responded by cladding his riders in long-sleeved, one-piece Lycra suits that covered the skin.

Dubbed the 'Chronosuit', the Assos skinsuit made its debut at the 1978 World Track Championships, and was so successful that by the 1980 Moscow Olympics every rider was wearing a skinsuit. By the 1984 Los Angeles Olympics, a handful of road racers were wearing them too.

One of the first to kit out his riders in skinsuits for the time-trial, or the 'race of truth' as it's known in cycling parlance, was Peter Post. A highly successful track and road rider who specialised in the one-day classics, the Dutchman went on to become one of the greatest team managers of all time at the helm of the TI-Raleigh team, which dominated team time-trialling in the 1970s and 1980s. Given that it's estimated that the 3.2 per cent energy saving provided by a body-hugging Lycra suit equates to 29 seconds over a 40km (25-mile) time-trial, it's little wonder that 'Panzer Group Post' were so dominant against the clock.

And it was no surprise that British Cycling, too, identified the skinsuit as a key part of their armoury when they went looking for marginal gains. In his book *Faster*, time-trial champion Michael Hutchinson makes the point that the best skinsuit delivers a greater aerodynamic advantage than upgrading to a better time-trial bike. When Mark Cavendish won the World Championships in 2011, he and his teammates wore skinsuits developed by British Cycling. It was unusual for a race team to wear suits, as they were previously the preserve of time-trials and track cyclists.

Skinsuits, though aerodynamic, aren't always the most comfortable gear to wear on a hot day. Enter the Rapha Road Race Mesh Skinsuit in 2014, which was designed to enable better airflow and to be both cooling and aerodynamic. Modelled by Chris Froome, when the somewhat see-through qualities of the suit were plain to see, the general opinion on Twitter was that here was a marginal gain too far. Another flaw was revealed when Froome suffered extremely bad sunburn while wearing it, although the suit is still worn (with suncream liberally applied to the skin underneath) in cooler early-season races. But perhaps we should all be grateful that a skinsuit, rather than nude cycling, turned out to be the most aerodynamic way of riding a bike...

Daniel Gisiger, racing for
Switzerland, shown wearing the
Assos 'Chronosuit', the first
skinsuit, at the 1978 World Track
Championships in Munich.

38 Heart rate monitor

Consisting of a chest strap containing electrodes that measure beats per minute coupled with a wristwatch-style receiver, the heart rate monitor allows athletes and coaches to increase the quality and efficiency of their training.

Training 'smarter not harder' is an idea popularised by the scientific approach of today's sports scene, but sports science itself is nothing new. In fact, its long history stretches right back to the 2nd century AD and the work of the Greek physician and philosopher Galen, who produced treatises on nutrition and fitness, even developing a series of strength exercises for athletes using prototype dumbbells, which probably would have been lead-loaded pieces of wood.

The development of exercise physiology, the discipline most closely related to modern sports science, dates back to the 1890s. By the 1900s 'repetition training' was in use by runners, and by the 1920s the term fartlek – from the Swedish *fart* (speed) and *lek* (play) – coined by Gösta Holmér was in use. The term 'interval training' was first used by German coach Woldemar Gerschler in the 1930s, which introduced the notion of training that stresses the body for short periods of time to improve performance. More importantly, it also aids recovery from that effort. Gerschler's methods – based on physiological principles – aimed to develop an athlete's cardiovascular capacity by creating a bigger, stronger heart.

The heart is the human engine room, and the heart rate – the number of times the heart beats in one minute – is one of the most accurate indicators of physical fitness. Yet cycling was relatively slow to benefit from advances in training methods based on sound scientific research that were being tested in other endurance sports at the time.

This is partly because the perceived route to cycling greatness had traditionally been to ride as hard and as far as possible. When Fausto Coppi was asked how cyclists could best progress, he replied *'Pedalare! Pedalare! Pedalare!'* or 'Ride! Ride! Ride!' It wasn't until the 1970s that coaches began to manually measure riders' heart rates and calculate their power outputs during interval training sessions on static bicycles (*see* pp. 86–87). A few years later, in the 1980s, the Italian professor Francesco Conconi first used rudimentary heart rate monitors to develop his 'Conconi test' to establish a rider's anaerobic threshold, and this pioneering work paved the way for a revolution in cycling training.

Put simply, the anaerobic threshold (AT) is the link between heart rate, intensity of exercise and a rider's performance ceiling. Once established, a rider can train to just below their AT for longer periods without tiring. In 1984, Conconi, who believed that training at AT could be sustained for around an hour, trained Francesco Moser for his successful hour record attempt using the test.

This was revolutionary – gone were the days of simply 'putting in the miles'; trainers and coaches now had a method of setting quantifiable goals for speed and power outputs. By determining a rider's AT, training programmes could be carefully calibrated to match their potential.

Moreover, Conconi had been an early adopter of the EKG (Elektrokardiagram, or ECG electrocardiogram) heart rate monitor developed by Seppo Säynäjäkangas in 1977 as a training aid for the Finnish cross-country skiing team. By 1983, a wireless model was in production, making the ability to establish anaerobic threshold available to all. The EKG heart rate monitor is now a standard item in every serious professional and amateur cyclist's training kit and wearable devices have brought heart rate monitoring to even the most casual cyclists.

39 SRM power meter

If heart rate monitors refined the way that cyclists trained, then power meters have taken that refinement to the next level. Until the 1980s, riders had relied on laboratory testing to measure performance. While pedalling a stationary bike had its advantages for trainers – offering standard test conditions and the ability to take accurate measurements – it was difficult for riders to determine whether those performances were being replicated on the road.

Enter Ulrich Schoberer, a German medical engineer with a passion for cycling. In 1986, frustrated by his inability to measure his own fitness and training improvements, Schoberer identified power as the only absolute constant that would give him the measurements he needed to assess his progress. Unlike heart rate, power is not susceptible to variables such as illness, weather (heart rates are higher in hotter weather), and race conditions. In addition, power is an accurate measure of the work rate of a cyclist, allowing them to refine their training methods for best results in competition.

But how best to measure the power output (measured in watts – the energy required to move a mass a certain distance in a known time) from his bicycle? Schoberer hit on a simple and elegant solution. He identified the bottom bracket of the bike as the most efficient place to take his power measurements, before frictional forces from the drivetrain could affect the readings, and he placed the first SRM (Schoberer Rad Meßtechnik or Schoberer Bike Measurement Technology) here, every component of which was constructed by Schoberer himself.

Debuting two years later, in 1986, the SRM powercrank was used by Greg LeMond, who was so impressed he wrote and thanked Schoberer with the words: 'I wish you had invented SRM when I won the jersey in 1983 in Switzerland, I would have won many more.' Another enthusiastic advocate was Francesco Conconi, the Italian sports scientist, who urged his riders to embrace the new technology. A few years later in Britain, Nicole Cooke was one of the first women riders to use an SRM in the 1990s to measure power output during specific interval training.

The system works by using a series of strain gauges in the crankset (the component of a bicycle drivetrain that drives the chain), which measures the torsional force being applied through the pedals. This is then combined with cadence measurement (the number of revolutions that the crank makes in one minute) and is expressed as a power measurement in watts. Though the earliest units were wired, readings are now transmitted wirelessly to the head unit mounted on the bike's handlebars. From there, readings can be downloaded to a computer for analysis, or these days even sent to TV companies to appear in live coverage.

Power meters are now a standard part of the 'marginal gains' toolkit, though their use offers a maximal gain, thanks to its impact on training. A specially designed SRM was even tested under zero gravity on the MIR space station. Despite its multiple uses, however, the system retains its essential simplicity. As its founder said: 'Watts are watts. The more watts the better, it's as simple as that.'

Jurgen Van den Broeck adjusts
his SRM power meter ahead of
the 2011 Vuelta a Andalucia.

40 Bicycle computer

Modern cyclists use on-bike computers to record everything from distance and speed to power and cadence, a facility that was made possible by Curtis Veeder when he invented his Cyclometer 150 years ago.

Veeder, born in 1862 in Pennsylvania, USA, was a prolific inventor. He built his first high-wheeler aged 18, then shortly afterwards patented a design for a bicycle saddle, the rights for which he eventually sold for US$1000. However, it is for the Cyclometer, which rolled off the production line of his Veeder Manufacturing Company in 1895, that he is best known.

The Cyclometer was a simple device consisting of an odometer – a device to measure distance travelled – attached to a star-shaped wheel that struck the spokes of the back wheel and measured the number of rotations made. These were then converted to distance readings. Often inaccurate, however, the Cyclometer was superseded in the mid-20th century by cable-driven speedometers that allowed cyclists to measure both speed and distance, albeit in a rudimentary fashion.

The 1970s saw a significant step forwards with the introduction of the Huret Multito. Driven by a rubber O-ring cable belt attached to the front axle, it was capable of recording both total distance and trip distance. However, the belt drive was susceptible to changes in temperature and humidity so what the device made up for in features, it sometimes lacked in accuracy.

The first real bike computer was the Avocet Cyclometer 20, launched in 1983 and made available commercially in 1985. A fully electronic device that could calculate speed, time and distance based on the number of times the wheel rotated, it weighed less than 30g (1oz) and was endorsed by world champion Greg LeMond. Avocet continues to produce cycling computers.

Since then, the bicycle computer has advanced to keep pace with modern technology and now comes packed with features, including GPS technology. Garmin has long been the market leader, producing the wrist-mounted Forerunner in the early 2000s and then the Edge bicycle computer range. In 2008, Garmin partnered with American team Slipstream-Chipotle and has continued to equip the team with cutting-edge technology. By 2016, Garmin technology was in use by the Cannondale, Movistar and Lampre–Merida teams and is a firm favourite with recreational cyclists.

Where once wheel circumference needed to be measured and test runs over known distances performed to ensure that the device was delivering the most accurate information possible, GPS-enabled computers now perform these calculations on the fly. The newest wireless technology for bike computers is ANT+ and Bluetooth, which allow interoperability between the computer and sensors such as heart rate monitors and power meters. Simple to use and expand by adding new sensors, users can quickly and easily access the data they need.

No system is foolproof, as was demonstrated in 2015 when Strava, the social network that allows cyclists to share their bicycle computer data, reported a rash of phantom cyclists using motorised bikes to record the fastest times on several iconic climbs. Cycling, it seems, will always attract its share of cheats.

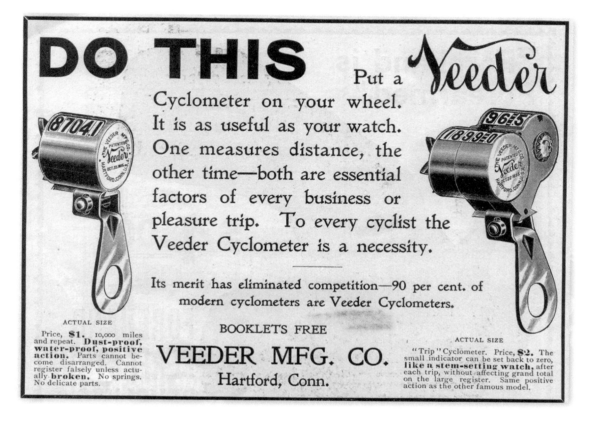

DO THIS Put a *Veeder*

Cyclometer on your wheel. It is as useful as your watch. One measures distance, the other time—both are essential factors of every business or pleasure trip. To every cyclist the Veeder Cyclometer is a necessity.

Its merit has eliminated competition—90 per cent. of modern cyclometers are Veeder Cyclometers.

BOOKLETS FREE

VEEDER MFG. CO.
Hartford, Conn.

ACTUAL SIZE

Price, **$1.** 10,000 miles and repeat. **Dust-proof, water-proof, positive action.** Parts cannot become disarranged. Cannot register falsely unless actually **broken.** No springs. No delicate parts.

ACTUAL SIZE

"Trip" Cyclometer. Price, **$2.** The small indicator can be set back to zero, **like a stem-setting watch,** after each trip, without affecting grand total on the large register. Same positive action as the other famous model.

An advertisement for the Veeder bicycle cyclometer, by the Veeder Manufacturing Company, circa 1899. The Veeder Cyclometer was the forerunner of the modern bike computer that can record everything from distance and speed to power and cadence.

41 Wind tunnel

In the 21st century, bicycle-component manufacturers and cycling teams routinely use wind tunnel technology to run aerodynamic testing, but the wind tunnel itself is much older, with roots in the fledgling aeronautics industry of the late 19th century.

The study of aerodynamics stretches back through history to the 2nd and 3rd centuries BC, and the work of Aristotle and Archimedes on airflow and resistance. Many centuries years later during the Enlightenment, the 17th and 18th century approach to aerodynamic testing followed two distinct methodologies. First, a model could either be placed in a steady flow of air, as might be found naturally in a cave mouth, or be moved through the air at speed. The second, more advanced, method was to use a whirling arm (a sort of aeronautical centrifuge) that was developed in the early 18th century and remained the standard until the 19th century. However, although this was more reliable than holding an item in natural air flow in a cave mouth, the action of the whirling arm as it spun round on a pivot created turbulence that rendered many measurements inaccurate. A better alternative was needed, which is where the wind tunnel comes in.

Frank H. Wenham of the Aeronautical Society of Great Britain is credited with building the first true wind tunnel in Greenwich, England, in 1871. Consisting of a tube 3.66m (12ft) long and with a diameter of 46cm² (18in²) down which air was propelled by a fan blower, this was to be the blueprint for all subsequent wind-tunnel facilities.

Aerodynamics play a huge part in bike racing, since reducing the frontal area of a rider allows them to move through the air with the least resistance possible. Yet as speed increases, so does a rider's effort to combat wind resistance – at 30kph (18.6mph) this equates to around 80 per cent of a rider's effort. The lower the resistance, the quicker a rider's speed will be, and wind-tunnel testing has become the norm for adjusting a rider's position to be as efficient as possible.

Despite the best efforts of Henri Desgrange to discourage riders in the early Tours de France from working together, the idea of riding in a tightly grouped pack or peloton quickly gained currency. Little wonder, since the energy saving for a rider tucked securely in the slipstream of another is as high as 40 per cent. However, for a rider making a solo effort, for example in an hour record attempt, the fight against drag becomes vitally important, which is why many – including Francesco Moser before his successful attempt on the record in Mexico City in 1984 – use wind-tunnel testing to fine-tune riding position.

But it was the French team Renault-Gitane and their innovative use of wind-tunnel testing in the 1970s and 1980s that made it a must-have technology. Renault saw both its cycling and Formula 1 sponsorship as a test bed for new technologies to be used in car manufacture and so made their biomechanical and aerodynamic expertise available to the team. After perfecting his position in the wind tunnel, team leader Bernard Hinault was calculated to have improved his efficiency in a time-trial by a significant two seconds per kilometre. As a result of this collaboration, Renault produced the Profil – a prototype aerodynamic bicycle on which Hinault would win all three long individual time-trials at the Tour de France before taking overall victory in 1979.

Today, wheels and aero bars, time-trialling helmets and skinsuits are all routinely wind-tunnel tested. Several teams have invested in their own facilities, and riders continue to use these to make minute adjustments to their position that may give them a race-winning advantage.

Peter Sagan, shown training in a wind tunnel to refine his positioning.

42 Radio communication

The arrival of the USA in the Tour de France peloton in the 1980s brought with it not only a new wave of competitors, but also their innovations, notably triathlon bars and race radios.

It's difficult to remember a time when a rider wasn't seen with a telltale piece of tape holding an earpiece in his ear, but they haven't been around especially long. The first to race using two-way radio communications between rider and team car was the American Motorola team – comprising a raft of English-speaking riders, such as Australian Phil Anderson, British Sean Yates, Canadian Steve Bauer and Americans Lance Armstrong and George Hincapie – in 1991.

For telecommunications firm Motorola the idea of equipping the team they sponsored with two-way radios was irresistible. Moreover, the phenomenal success of Lance Armstrong – who took radio technology with him when he moved to the US Postal team in 1998 – only hastened the spread of radio use throughout the peloton. With race radios allowing team directors far greater control over race tactics, the complexion of road cycling changed overnight.

For 100 years, communication between a rider and his team manager had taken place either at the dinner table or by talking through the open window of a team car. More recently, race radio, the official communications' channel of the Tour, had broadcast information regarding time gaps and incidents on the road, though only in French. If the peloton wanted to catch a breakaway they were forced to rely on time gaps marked up on the chalkboard carried on the back of a motorbike and their own instincts to work out how to do so. Race radios, by contrast, allowed team directors to calculate precisely the position of riders on

the road, the time gaps between them, and the precise effort needed to make the catch.

Perhaps the most famous use of the technology came in the 2001 Tour de France, when Armstrong's *directeur sportif* tactically let it be known over race radio that his star rider was not feeling well. Hearing the news, the team of his great German rival, Jan Ulrich, was ordered to the front of the peloton and led the race through kilometre after kilometre of a tough stage in the Alps. Finally, at the foot of Alpe d'Huez, the American surged to the head of the peloton and took a long, hard look at Ulrich before pedalling away for a decisive win. The 'Look' has since entered the annals of Tour de France history.

Riders and team managers are in favour of the use of radios. It makes the sport safer, they say, allowing the team car to disseminate important information about hazards on the route quickly and effectively. The naysayers, meanwhile, protest that it has robbed riders of their own ability to think and react for themselves as they wait for team instructions, with the result that races are becoming less exciting, unfolding tactically in set and predictable patterns.

The UCI first moved to ban race radios in 2011, after French television executives threatened the race with a reduction in coverage if they weren't removed. The UCI has since experimented with banning radios on certain stages of the Tour, and in certain races at non-elite level of cycling, to little obvious effect. A total ban was mooted for the 2015 cycling season, until the UCI climbed down in the face of team protests. However, although radio technology remains banned in several races, including the World Championships and the Tour of Britain, it seems that race radios may be in the peloton to stay.

Mark Cavendish, wearing the points leader's jersey, shown adjusting his radio at the 2016 Tour of Dubai.

Contrôl
Anti-Dopag

Doping

43 Amphetamines

James Edward 'Choppy' Warburton was born in Lancashire, England, in 1864. A flamboyant showman, Warburton had been a record-breaking runner in his youth before he switched to cycle coaching in the 1890s and became infamous for the little black bottle from which he would pour some mysterious liquid that he'd give to his cyclists when they were flagging. One of his protégés was Welshman Arthur Linton, who became cycling's first reported doping casualty when he overdosed on a substance known as 'trimethyl' (an alcohol-based stimulant) just two weeks after his success in Paris–Bordeaux in 1886.

By the time the famous Pélissier brothers sat down with journalist Albert Londres in a small French café in 1924, doping in cycling was widespread, as was revealed by the sensational interview that followed. Huddled around that café table, Henri and Francis proceeded to reveal the sordid secrets of professional cycling. 'What do you take?' Londres had enquired. 'Everything!' exclaimed Henri: 'That's cocaine for the eyes, that's chloroform for the gums – and the pills, do you want to see the pills? Here, these are the pills. Basically, we ride on dynamite.'

By the 1930s, there was a new drug of choice in the peloton: amphetamines. First synthesised in 1897, these were not finally licenced for therapeutic use until 1937. Use in the military became widespread during World War II, both as a means of combatting fatigue and to psych up soldiers before dangerous and deadly combat missions.

Amphetamines quickly replaced strychnine, which had been used to tighten tired muscles, as the preferred stimulant for professional cyclists. Fausto Coppi was reported to have used 'seven packets of amphetamines' for his hour record attempt in 1942 and made little secret of the fact that he used 'la Bomba' – a combination of Coca-Cola, cocaine and amphetamines – throughout his career. The first five-time Tour de France winner Jacques Anquetil also used them, though he claimed they were used more for overall recovery than for gains in speed.

Despite their apparent advantages in terms of performance, the side effects and the risks involved were considerable. This was highlighted in 1955 when French rider Jean Malléjac collapsed and nearly died on Mont Ventoux during the Tour de France. Five years later, at the 1960 Rome Olympics, Danish cyclist Knut Jensen collapsed and died after the 100km time-trial. The autopsy discovered traces of amphetamines in his bloodstream.

One of the sport's greatest tragedies was the death of Britain's Tom Simpson in 1967. Like Malléjac, he collapsed on Mont Ventoux; unlike Malléjac, he died on the barren slopes of the Bald Mountain, caught in a perfect storm of amphetamines, alcohol and heat exhaustion. His death became the catalyst for greater efforts to combat the widespread problems of doping in sport, partly because those awful events were screened on live television.

The official race doctor Pierre Dumas, who had attended to both Simpson and Malléjac, had campaigned hard for drug testing in the sport and, in 1966, France passed what became known as Herzog's Law, after the Minister for Sport and Youth, Maurice Herzog. The first cyclist tested at the Tour was Raymond Poulidor, dubbed the 'Eternal Second' since he never won the race. However, perhaps predictably, fellow riders were unhappy with this intrusion into their private practices and went on strike, which resulted in it being another decade before effective testing began and another 32 years before the World Anti-Doping Agency was formed in 1999. All of this was too late for Simpson of course, whose tragic death is memorialised on the slopes of Mont Ventoux.

Five times Tour de France winner Jacques
Anquetil claimed he used amphetamines for
recovery, not speed. He smiles as he rides
around the track of the Parc des Princes in
Paris, following his first victory in 1957.

44 EPO ampoule

The drug Erythropoietin (EPO) works by raising a rider's red blood cell count, transporting more oxygen to the bloodstream, increasing aerobic capacity and the ability to resist fatigue. In 2007, a study published in the *European Journal of Applied Physiology* showed that EPO use by a group of fit amateur cyclists improved their peak power output by 13 per cent. The implications for an elite Grand Tour rider are therefore huge.

This was clearly demonstrated in 1996 when, at the age of 32, Bjarne Riis became the first Danish rider to win the Tour de France, cementing his victory with an extraordinary display on the climb of the Hautacam. In 2007, Riis – who had a solid if unspectacular 10-year career as a professional cyclist – admitted that his victory had been fuelled by a cocktail of performance-enhancing drugs, including EPO. Dutch cyclist Johannes Draaijer was not so lucky. He died of a heart attack in 1990 at the age of 26. Draaijer's death was just one of a string of fatalities linked to EPO, whose prolonged use thickens the blood to the consistency of jam and can cause cardiac arrest as the heart struggles to pump it around the body.

In response, cycling authorities sought a way of monitoring EPO use by testing cyclists' blood. Whole blood is composed of red blood cells and plasma and the ratio of the volume of red blood cells to whole blood is referred to as the haematocrit (HCT) level. It was this that the UCI seized upon as a way to curtail EPO use, setting a maximum HCT level of 50 per cent in 1998.

Ironically, that year also saw one of the most notorious doping scandals in cycling history: the Festina affair. This involved riders of the Festina team being ejected from the Tour de France following the discovery by French customs officials before the race started of hundreds of ampoules of EPO in a car driven by Willy Voet, one of the team's soigneurs. The race was marred by a series of police raids, rider strikes and team withdrawals. The eventual winner, Italy's Marco Pantani, was later discovered to have used EPO during the race.

Although the Festina riders all eventually confessed to taking EPO and were banned from riding for a short time, and the team manager and other personnel were handed suspended sentences, the affair rumbled on until 2000, by which time an American rider called Lance Armstrong – a promising classics rider and the youngest-ever world champion – had transformed himself into a Grand Tour rider and already won the Tour de France twice.

By the time testing for EPO was introduced at the Sydney Olympics, in 2000, it had already been widely used in professional cycling for over a decade. And drug-use remained rife, giving riders the edge that enabled them to go further, faster. Most infamous of these was Armstrong, who would go on to 'win' the Tour seven times before being stripped of his titles by the UCI in 2012 as a result of the US Anti-Doping Agency's Reasoned Decision, which stated that: 'the US Postal Service Pro Cycling Team ran the most sophisticated, professionalized and successful doping program that sport has ever seen.'

In a further attempt to put a stop to doping, in 2009 WADA approved the use of the Athlete Biological Passport (ABP) – a series of longitudinal tests that are compared to a rider's physiological baseline, and designed to combat the use of blood doping, including EPO. This has since been adopted by many international federations and anti-doping agencies across sport as a whole and will hopefully mark the end of a dismal chapter in the sport's history.

Lance Armstrong undergoing a doping
control test at the 2004 Tour de France.
He was stripped of his seven wins for
doping offences in 2012.

45 Urine test

The urine test, whereby a sample collected under strict conditions is analysed at a World Anti-Doping Agency (WADA) accredited laboratory, is one of the simplest weapons in the anti-doping arsenal.

The first urine tests carried out at a major sporting event anywhere in the world were conducted during the 1965 Tour of Britain and were initially performed to detect amphetamine use. Three years later, after Tom Simpson's very public death during the 1967 Tour de France, the International Olympic Committee (IOC) introduced drug testing at the Winter and Summer Olympic Games.

One of the first high-profile athletes to fail a urine test was Ben Johnson after testosterone was detected in a sample taken following a blistering run in the 100m event at the 1988 Seoul Olympics. Others followed, with the result that some athletes and their managers devised various means of cheating the test. These included Irish swimmer Michelle Smith – winner of three golds at the 1996 Atlanta Games – who was found to have a lethal level of alcohol in one of her urine samples in 1998. This, it transpired, was because Smith, who would later be banned from the sport for using performance-enhancing drugs, had deliberately contaminated a sample with whisky.

Cyclists were not immune to falsifying tests, either. During the 1978 Tour de France, Michel Pollentier, wearing the leader's yellow jersey, tried to fool testers by using a condom filled with another rider's urine. The ruse was discovered when the tester asked Pollentier to take off his jersey. Learning from Pollentier's mistakes, riders became more expert at concealing these samples, hiding the plastic tubing in their pubic hair. Other methods for cheating the urine test included rubbing household laundry powder on the hands or foreskin before urinating (the powder contains an enzyme called protease, which breaks down EPO) or simply micro-dosing with a banned substance to avoid detection.

In an attempt to stamp out such practices, WADA developed strict guidelines for urine testing to ensure a secure chain of custody of the urine sample. The process is an intrusive one, requiring that the doping control officer (DCO) – who must be the same gender as the athlete – witnesses the passing of urine. Before this is done, however, the person being tested is required to strip naked between mid-chest and mid-thigh so that the DCO can check for concealed samples. They then have a choice about which secure collection kit is to be used and will observe every stage of the sample-taking to ensure there are no irregularities. The athlete may also choose to be accompanied by a representative throughout the sample-taking procedure. Once the sample has been collected, the athlete personally seals the bottle immediately and is then allowed to get dressed.

In order to prevent drug use during training periods, urine testing may take place both in and out of competition. To this end, athletes must notify testers of their whereabouts and availability for out-of-competition testing through the Anti-Doping Administration & Management System (ADAMS). If an athlete fails to be at the stated location at the specified time, this may count as a missed test.

Despite WADA's best efforts, however, cyclists continue to pass drug tests even when they are subsequently proven to have taken performance-enhancing drugs. The most well-known example is Lance Armstrong, again, who claimed to have passed hundreds of tests during his cycling career.

Chris Froome enters the Anti-Doping Control centre during the 2013 Tour de France.

Cycling For All

46 Bicycle-club badge

Bicycle clubs offer their members more than just the opportunity to hone their cycling skills – they are hubs of social activity, open to all ages, which allow cycling to transcend the mechanics of pushing the pedals.

The Pickwick Bicycle Club, formed in London in 1870, claims to be the oldest cycling club in the world, a trend that accelerated as the bicycle craze swept the globe in the late 19th century, with many more associations for keen amateur cyclists popping up across Europe and the USA. Despite their image as easy-going groups of like-minded cyclists, these clubs were not, however, open to all. The bicycle may have been key to the emancipation of women, but women were not widely accepted in cycling clubs of the period. Instead, they established their own associations, with the Lady Cyclists' Association, formed in 1892, being one of the earliest – annual membership for which cost 3/6d (95¢). By 1900, however, there were hundreds of women's cycling clubs across the UK.

In America, membership tended to be split along racial and ethnic lines, with New York alone hosting Italian, German, Belgian and Irish cycling clubs. Nationwide, owing to pressure from members in the Southern states, the League of American Wheelmen would exclude black members in the 1890s, thus effectively barring them from racing. In his birthplace, Indianapolis, Major Taylor – the great black track rider who had become the first American cycling world champion – was thus forced to ride for the See-Saw Club, formed by black riders in 1895 in response to the whites-only Zig-Zag Cycling Club.

More specialist cycling clubs also sprung up, including the Vegetarian Cycling and Athletic Club, in the UK in 1888, which sought to prove that non-meat eaters could be just as competitive as their carnivorous fellows. They still welcome vegetarian athletes today. The Kent-based San Fairy Ann Cycling Club – which took its name from the French expression '*ça ne fait rien*'/'it means nothing', a popular catchphrase among British troops in World War I – was formed in the 1920s with the aim of benefitting ex-servicemen. Other clubs, such as the National Clarion Cycling Club in the UK and the Solidarity Worker Cycling Club in Germany, had a political bent and hoped to harness the new-found mobility of the working classes. The Solidarity Worker Cycling Club in particular was a significant socialist movement and by 1930 it had over 300,000 members, making it the biggest sporting association in the world at the time. Recognising the threat, it was banned by the Nazis in 1933.

The current rise in the popularity of cycling – chiming as it does with modern interests in health and well-being and environmental issues – has seen the humble cycling club rise again. Membership of British cycling clubs more than doubled between 2008 and 2016 and, in the same period, 20 million more Americans got on their bikes. In the Netherlands 99.1 per cent of the population now owns a bike, and many belong to a cycling group.

These days, members don't need to physically go to a club. Online groups such as iCycle and The Underachievers' Online Cycling Club, to name but a few, connect members from around the world through social media at Strava (*see* pp. 128–129), and women-only cycling clubs such as the Chester Fabulous Ladies in the UK, Black Girls Do Bike in the US, and the global site Ride Like a Girl are growing in popularity.

These modern clubs, even those that operate from a cyber platform rather than a building, continue to retain the original social function of the early cycling clubs, in developing friendship and community spirit as well as developing the sport.

SPRINGFIELD BICYCLE CLUB.

BICYCLE CAMP-EXHIBITION & TOURNAMENT.
SPRINGFIELD, MASS. U.S.A. SEPT. 18.19.20. 1883.

A poster dating from 1883 shows
crowds gathered for a meeting of the
Springfield Bicycle Club in
Massachusetts, USA. The first
cycling club was founded in 1870 and
interest in cycling club membership
is rising again in the 21st century.

47 Cycle paths

The Dutch are renowned for their extensive cycling infrastructure and love of a life on two wheels, but few know that it took furious public protest and the tragic deaths of 400 children on the roads in one year to bring about the cycling nirvana that is the Netherlands today.

At the turn of the 20th century, cycling was at the height of its popularity, and in Los Angeles alone 20 per cent of all traffic in 1900 was bicycles. Cyclists enjoyed the benefit of elevated cycling paths – a dedicated route running parallel to a road, as opposed to a painted lane on the highway – alongside other bike-friendly measures. Many of these first cycle paths were constructed in the Netherlands, although the 1894 Brooklyn Ocean Parkway in the USA – the first dedicated cycle path in North America and still in existence today – is believed to be the oldest in the world. Elsewhere, networks opened up all over the place. This trend for travelling by bicycle was to be short-lived, however, as the inexorable rise of the motorcar gradually eroded its dominance and cars became the go-to mode of transport. Los Angeles is now one of the most traffic-dense cities in the world.

The 1920s saw a boom in the construction of bicycle paths in Germany and legislation was passed that forced cyclists to use them. Although undoubtedly beneficial, the real motive for building a dedicated bike infrastructure both in Germany and elsewhere was less about providing a safe and comfortable cycling experience and more about discouraging cyclists from using the roads and getting in the way of cars. As was noted at the first Dutch Road Congress in 1920: 'the construction of bicycle paths along the larger roads relieves traffic along these roads of an extremely bothersome element: the cyclist.'

By the end of World War II, the availability of cheap cars coupled with a rise in prosperity saw an inexorable growth in the popularity of motor transport. Cycling correspondingly went into a decline in the UK and the USA. In the Netherlands, too, cycling waned in popularity – not helped by the decisions of urban planners who razed to the ground entire neighbourhoods of Amsterdam to make way for motorised traffic, so convinced were they that the motorcar was the future of transportation.

In the 20 years from 1950 to 1970, traffic fatalities rose alarmingly in the Netherlands, far outstripping road deaths in the UK. In response, angry citizens formed the Stop de Kindermoord (Stop the Child Murder) movement, which organised bicycle protests and blockaded roads to allow children to play safely. When the oil crisis hit in 1973 and the price of petrol quadrupled, the Dutch government declared a series of car-free Sundays and the Dutch began to rediscover the pleasures of a quiet bicycle ride. By the 1980s, The Hague was one of the first Dutch cities to experiment with a network of cycle paths, and others followed rapidly. Today, there are 357,275km (220,000 miles) of bike paths in the Netherlands and at least a quarter of all trips are made by bicycle. In the UK, that figure stands at just 2 per cent.

Things did improve in the UK too, though, and in 1995, with the support of Lottery funding, the National Cycle Network opened its first bike path. There are now more than 22,530km (14,000 miles) of signposted cycle routes in the UK.

Two cyclists pass under a sculpture known as The Pencils by Derek Morrison on the 14-mile stretch of cycle path between Bristol and Bath, UK. Cycle paths have made cycling safer for all.

Although the Brompton has become the instantly recognisable face of the modern folding bicycle, its history actually starts in 1887 when American inventor Emmit G. Latta filed a patent to construct a bicycle: 'in such a manner that the same can be folded when not required for use, so as to require little storage-room and facilitate its transportation.' Then, in 1893, another American, Michael B. Ryan, also filed for a patent for a folding bicycle, swiftly followed by Frenchmen Julien Simon and Victor Dussault, who invented the folding tandem in 1895.

Despite this, credit for inventing the folding bike is given, however erroneously, to the French military and one Captain Gérard. He had originally filed a patent for a folding bike for military use in 1893, but the design was completely impractical. Enter Charles Morel, a wealthy industrialist who had filed a patent for his own version of the folding bike a year earlier. Morel agreed to collaborate with Gérard – he would finance and produce the bike and the army man would promote it. The first folding bike subsequently rolled off the production line in April 1895 and a store in Paris opened in October that year.

As the public face of the folding bike Gérard succeeded in selling models to the French, Russian and Romanian armies, and was put in charge of a regiment equipped with 'his' folding bikes, earning himself the rank of Captain in the process. Perceived by the general public to be the inventor of the machine, Gérard soon began to believe his own publicity and sued Morel for his fair share of the profits. Their partnership ended in acrimony and a consortium of Peugeot, Michelin and the French Army took over production in 1889, meaning that although falsely attributed, the 'Captain Gérard folding

bike' did succeed where others had failed, becoming the first-mass produced folding bicycle.

These early (and many subsequent) models used conventional diamond-frame geometry with a central hinge, which Andrew Ritchie overturned when he designed the Brompton in 1975. Ritchie's main innovation was to create an origami fold that would allow both wheels to come to the centre on each side of the chain wheel, thus protecting users from the dirtiest part of the bicycle when carrying it. Ritchie had taken his inspiration from the Bickerton – a portable aluminium bike designed by Henry Bickerton and produced between 1971 and 1989. With its small wheels yet standard-height seat post and handlebars, this was a fine starting point in the search for the 'ultimate in compactness', a quest that Ritchie undertook in a flat overlooking the Brompton Oratory in London, hence the name.

Rejected by major bicycle manufacturers such as Raleigh, Ritchie instead founded his own company and small-scale production began in 1981, growing over the years and becoming mass produced in 1988. It's success continued unabated thereafter, and in 1995 Brompton received the Queen's Award for Export Achievement.

Popular with commuters for their portability and tiny footprint – it takes just a few seconds to fold the bike into a package about 61cm² (2ft²) – Bromptons have been ridden around the globe, including to the South Pole in 2003, and held their inaugural World Championships in 2006, in Barcelona. Competitors have included Commonwealth champion cyclist Michael Hutchinson and Vuelta a España winner Roberto Heras, both of whom abided by the strict dress code of jacket, tie and absolutely no Lycra.

Two participants abiding by the strict and stylish dress code of jacket and tie at the Brompton World Championships at Goodwood Motor Circuit in 2013. The Brompton folding bicycle is particularly popular with commuters as its unique origami fold makes it easily portable.

49 Vélib' bike-sharing scheme

From Amsterdam's Witte Fietsenplan (White Bicycle plan) to the Boris Bikes on the streets of London, bike-share schemes have overcome their teething problems to provide healthier, greener, cleaner transport for city dwellers across the globe.

The White Bicycle plan – started as a protest by Dutch counterculture group Provo – is probably the most influential bike-sharing scheme that never happened. Developed in 1965 as a reaction to a proposal to allow more cars on to the narrow streets of Amsterdam, the White Bicycle plan would instead have put 20,000 bikes on the streets, for free usage. Though the proposal was rejected by the authorities and never put into official operation (although the group did paint 50 bicycles white and made them available for public use, until they were impounded), it directly influenced the Yellow Bike Project (YBP) that started in Portland, Oregon, in 1994.

The Copenhagen Bycyklen project, also launched in 1994, used a simple coin-deposit scheme that was meant to deter theft and incentivise the return of bicycles. Unlike the Yellow Bike scheme, the Copenhagen bikes were purpose-designed with solid components and advertising plates that could be used to finance the scheme. In addition, they could be collected and dropped off at designated stations, streamlining the system.

The next generation of bike-sharing programmes was developed at Portsmouth University in England. Bikeabout, introduced in 1996, involved the use of a magnetic swipe card to rent a bike. A similar scheme was tried in Rennes, France, two years later. Called Vélo à La Carte, this used smart-card access to gather information on users' cycling patterns, allowing providers to ensure that bikes were in the right place at the right time. Cyclists were also entitled to 30 minutes' free riding, encouraging their use for short trips.

Though the Parisian Vélib' bike-share scheme is the third-biggest in the world – and the largest outside China – it was the Vélo'v scheme launched in Lyon in 2005 that was the catalyst for successful city bike-sharing schemes. Until the implementation of Vélo'v as part of a raft of cycle-friendly schemes in the city, only 1.5 per cent of trips had been made by bike. In just three years, that figure jumped by 500 per cent to 7.5 per cent, driven by the success of the Vélo'v scheme, saving an estimated 7300 tons of CO_2 emissions.

Despite this, it was Paris' Vélib' – from the French *vélo* for 'bicycle' and *liberté* for 'freedom' – that has become the benchmark for all successful city bike-sharing schemes. Proving that cycling is not just a pastime but a serious form of transport, Vélib' users can avoid gridlock and parking problems while at the same time helping to negate pollution problems in the French capital.

Vélib' launched on the French national holiday, Bastille Day, in July 2007. By the fifth anniversary of the scheme, 138 million people had used the distinctive chunky silver bikes. Though relatively expensive to administer, the programme started to turn a profit in 2011 and problems of bike availability have been solved by the development of Vélib' apps.

Since then, the scheme has spread: 31 Parisian suburbs and 34 French towns now run bike-sharing schemes based on the Parisian model and Vélib' has inspired similar successful initiatives around the world, from Melbourne to San Francisco and the Boris Bikes in London.

The Vélib' bicycle-sharing scheme
was launched in Paris in 2015. The
Vélib' is the clean, green and healthy
way to get around the French capital.

Home trainer

The sight of professional riders warming up and cooling down on stationary bikes is now a familiar one, and both pro and keen amateur cyclists alike have long spent their winter months keeping fit on indoor cycling devices such as rollers and turbo trainers.

The first rudimentary bicycle trainer actually pre-dates the first bicycle. Called the Gymnasticon, it was invented in 1796 by Englishman Francis Lowndes – a pioneer in the field of medical electricity as a therapy and cure for injury and disease – to exercise the joints and muscles, and consisted of two large wheels mounted on a frame and propelled by hand cranks and foot treadles.

Bicycle trainers based on the high-wheeler and safety bicycles were already in use when Albert Schlock, an American who rode the US and European six-day circuits, developed his training wheel in the 1890s, on which he claimed to be able to cover a mile in less than three minutes. Schlock's trainer, essentially a saddle mounted on a pedal-driven flywheel, was the precursor of exercise bicycles familiar in any modern gym.

Another early type of stationary bicycle, the ergometer, was developed with the specific purpose of testing a user's work rate rather than just as a training vehicle. Refined in the 1950s, they were in common use in the 1970s as a way of measuring a cyclist's power output and heart rate and are still used in sports physiology labs. Rollers, devices that typically consist of a system of three rollers held in a frame on which a rider balances their bike and cycles, have also been popular since the height of the bicycle boom at the end of the 19th century. Both the turbo and roller styles of home trainer allow cyclists to exercise indoors without the distraction of other road users. Whereas the turbo trainer builds strength and power by working against resistance, rollers force a rider to focus on cadence and technique.

Another variation on indoor training is the spin bike. Developed by keen endurance cyclist Jonathan Goldberg, the spin bike made its debut in the 1990s and represents the culmination of his quest to develop a home-trainer that more closely replicated what happened on the open road. A fixed-gear stationary bike with a weighted flywheel and adjustable tension, the spin bike can simulate climbing as well as riding flat, and soon became an exercise phenomenon. Goldberg opened his first spin studio in a disused garage in California in 1987, and just a year later more than a million people had taken part in a spin class at their gym. By 1993, *Rolling Stone* magazine was calling spinning the 'hot' new exercise craze.

The most recent arrival on the stationary bike scene is Rollapaluza. This jazzily named machine has revived the sport of indoor roller racing and involves two or more competitors racing each other on stationary bikes in timed events. Although not entirely new – the world's only roller-racing professional, Britain's Eddie Wingrave, toured theatres with a big band in the 1950s, challenging members of the audience to come on stage and try to beat him, Rollapaluza brings it right into the 21st century with races taking place in pubs (where the craze originated), shopping centres and parks, complete with loud music, MCs and cheering crowds, as well as in schools.

For riders who still prefer to grind out their training efforts alone, there are clever ways to alleviate the boredom. Zwift is a turbo trainer game that allows riders to link up to a device, immersing them in a virtual world where they can ride with other riders with measurable results. The daddy of them all, the Sufferfest, has a range of video workouts that allow you to train with performance targets in real race environments like the Tour de France.

The original 1798 patent for the Gymnasticon,
invented by Francis Lowndes, a machine for
exercising the joints and muscles of the
human body. This was the forerunner of the
modern exercise bike and home trainer.

PATENT GYMNASTICON

or, Machine for Exercising the Joints & Muscles of the human Body.

51 Bicycle lamp

The Vienna Convention on Road Safety (1993) states that all bicycles used in member countries of the UN Economic Commission for Europe (UNECE) must have working brakes, an audible bell, a red reflector at the rear, and a white or yellow light visible at the front. Across Europe, the UK, the USA, as well as elsewhere, national legislation exists that governs the legal requirements for cycle lights in each specific country.

Every responsible cyclist wants to see and be seen when riding at night or in poor weather conditions. A bicycle light needs to be clearly visible to other traffic and pedestrians as well as lighting the road ahead so the cyclist can see where they are going. Crucially, it should also stay lit when the rider has come to a stop. Modern cyclists use ultra-bright light-emitting diodes (LEDs) coupled with rear-mounted reflectors to ensure their bikes are legally compliant, but in the days of the 'ordinary', long before safety legislation, a cyclist would light their way at night with an adapted carriage lantern powered by candlelight, and later oil or kerosene.

The first bicycle lamps from the 1860s were based on oil-burning carriage lanterns. These were often ornate affairs, made of brass with red and green jewels to indicate the left and right sides of the machine, an idea taken from the port and starboard indicators used on boats. The problem with the front-mounted lamps was the unpleasant fumes they emitted straight into the cyclist's face, and by the 1870s hub lamps were in vogue. These were square in shape, with a hinged barrel that fitted snugly over the axle hub of a high-wheeler.

Two major innovations saw electricity firmly installed as the way forward for bicycle lamps. First, the dry-cell battery, in 1889, which could power a bicycle lamp for 20 hours, and second the introduction of the cheaper tungsten filament bulb (the earliest bulbs had used fragile and costly carbon filaments) in 1911. These remain in production to this day, although the type of battery changed when the modern alkaline battery was introduced in the 1950s.

An alternative to gas or battery lamps are ones powered instead by the rider. Dynamos have been around since the 1890s, and it was the bottle-shaped dynamo that changed the game for bicycle lighting. Effectively a tiny generator using magnets to produce electricity that was built into the bicycle hub, a bottle dynamo could power a front lamp, as patented by German Rudolf Frauenfelder in 1919. The design caught on, and in Germany dynamo lights are still designed to comply with the country's strict safety lighting regulations, which meant that until 2013 battery-powered lights remained illegal there. In the UK, it was the Sturmey-Archer Dynohub – first introduced in the 1930s – that popularised dynamo-driven bike lamps. Simple and silent, with no moving parts or friction, a Dynohub is nevertheless capable of powering modern LED lights.

Advances in bulb, lens-optic, battery and magnet technology have all contributed to the bicycle-lighting revolution too. The introduction of halogen bulbs in the 1980s was a huge leap forwards, producing a powerful beam that improved cyclists' safety, but this came at a price: halogens were power hungry, relying on rechargeable batteries or dynamos to drive them, so they were soon supplanted by LEDs. Though the red LED was first utilised in the 1960s, it was the invention of blue and white LEDs in the 1990s that paved the way for their widespread use. Tiny, lightweight and power-efficient, LED white lights (front) and red lights (rear) are now standard on bikes around the world.

114

An advert for a acetylene gas-powered
bicycle lamp by the Plume and Atwood
Manufacturing Company in New York,
1897. The bicycle lamp has helped cyclists
be safe and be seen since the 1860s.

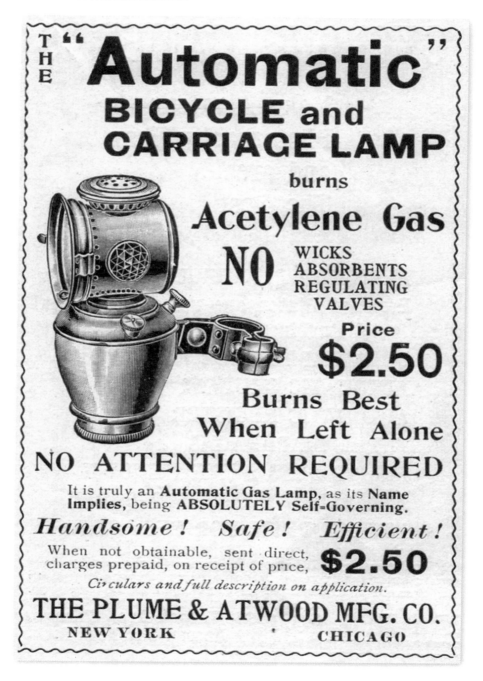

52 Hi-vis jacket

The history of hi-vis clothing began, by accident, one summer in 1933, with a man called Bob Switzer, some minerals and a darkened room.

Nineteen-year-old Switzer, who planned to become a doctor, was working in a pickle factory when he fell and hit his head, sending him into a coma from which he would eventually emerge with impaired memory and damaged eyesight. Confined to his parents' darkened basement to let his eyes recover, Bob, and his brother, Joe, a budding magician, amused themselves by using naturally fluorescing minerals to produce effects for Joe's magic shows. Once Bob had recovered, the brothers started experimenting by mixing the minerals with wood varnish, and thus produced the world's first day-glo colours, which are visible to the naked eye in daylight.

Spotting the potential for their paint, the so-called 'Day-glo Brothers' started selling it to other magicians, and for use on advertising displays and movie posters. Before long, the US military got wind of it, and the brothers subsequently saw their fluorescent colours used by the military for night flights and for signalling purposes – in North Africa troops used day-glo fabric panels to identify themselves as 'friendlies'. Post-war, the brothers' signature colour 'Blaze Orange' was adopted by US aeroplanes for better visability to help avoid collisions.

The applications for the day-glo paint and the fabric the Switzers had subsequently developed were endless – from tennis balls to traffic cones to Pop Art – and the paint and fabric soon spread across the world. In the UK, the most obvious application of the technology was the now-ubiquitous hi-vis jacket, which arrived in the 1960s on the Scottish railways and went on to be synonymous with the rise of 'health and safety' culture that ensued, with government legislation of the 1990s making its use compulsory for many occupations.

In the realm of recreational cycling, the use of hi-vis vests to make cyclists more conspicuous seems advantageous, one would think. However, some campaigners in the UK argue the exact opposite – claiming that by highlighting cyclists you are sending the message that cycling is an inherently unsafe activity. Moreover, the perception that cycling is risky is the greatest barrier to getting more people on their bikes and, even worse, hi-vis may breed a sense of complacency.

Then there are the studies into motorcycling that have been conducted since the late 1960s, which conclude that although a rider may be more visible in a hi-vis jacket, they are no more so than when they are clad in a white or black one: 'the most conspicuous outfit will be dictated by the lighting conditions and local environment at the time, which may be extremely variable within the confines of even a fairly short ride.' With the prevalence of workmen in hi-visibility jackets on UK roads, it is also possible that cyclists may get lost in the general visual noise.

So, what's the alternative? Campaigners suggest that a real change in attitudes to the provision of cycling infrastructure – as has happened in north-west European countries such as the Netherlands and Denmark (where hi-vis is not compulsory) – would make cycling safer than the wearing of hi-vis clothing. Elsewhere in Europe, though, the bright vests and jackets are mandatory for cycling in poor light conditions, and in the event of your car breaking down – a message that was highlighted in France with the release of a public-safety information film in 2008 in which designer Karl Lagerfeld, clad in hi-vis, declared: 'It's yellow, it's ugly. It doesn't go with anything, but it could save your life.' There is, it seems, no 'one size fits all' solution – not even a hi-vis jacket.

'It's yellow, it's ugly. It doesn't go with anything, but it could save your life.' Karl Lagerfeld brings high fashion to hi-vis as part of an advertising campaign for road safety in France.

53 Bicycle pump

Though the days when a professional cyclist had to fix their own punctures and inflate their own tyres are long gone, the bicycle pump remains a standard piece of equipment for the commuter and leisure rider who doesn't have the benefit of riding with a support car.

When Dunlop first inflated the tyres he had invented for his son's tricycle, he used a football pump. Invented in the 1860s by Robert Lindon, the pump was based on the principle of an ear syringe, which in itself was nothing new, since similar piston syringes had been in use since Roman times.

The bicycle pump is basically an adaptation of the football pump that has been fitted with a suitable valve to force the air into the tyre. When the handle is extended, air is sucked through an intake valve and into the pump. Depressing the handle forces the air out of the pump. A plunger assembly inside the tube ensures that all the air is evacuated from the pump cylinder.

The Welch-Dunlop hand pump was in use by the 1890s, but patents for many adaptations were filed during the period of the great bicycle boom, when inventors turned their attention to refining every aspect of a bicycle's design. Such innovators included John Braun, who designed and patented a pump that could double as a bike stand in the 1890s. In the same period, patents were filed for telescopic pumps and even automatic pumps that kept the wheel constantly inflated while in motion. In 1901, Melvin F. Rock filed a patent for a pump housed in the seat-post tube. The ingenious design turned the seat post tube into a fully integrated pump, operated by means of a detachable handle fitted in place of the saddle, and worked like a floor pump. Modern developments include a bike pump/bicycle lock combination and a pump that doubles as tyre-repair apparatus.

In order to allow a jet of air to be directed into it or for air to be able to come out of it, the bicycle tyre needed a valve. Cue August Schrader, a German emigrant in New York, who created the Schrader valve in the 1890s. Also known as the 'American valve', it is still in use today on all entry-level bicycles, children's bikes, mountain bikes and cars. Most road bikes, where tyres are inflated to a higher pressure, use a Presta or 'French valve'. Slimmer and taller than the Schrader, the Presta was patented in the 1920s and is more suitable for bikes with thinner rims.

Although the frame-mounted, hand-held bicycle pump is still around, most serious cyclists now prefer to use a floor or track pump to inflate their tyres, and carry a mini or hand pump or a CO_2 inflator for emergencies. Whatever the type used, however, there is no doubt that for any cyclist interested in maintaining their equipment, a decent pump is an essential tool.

The bicycle pump – the cyclist's best friend whenever a puncture happens. The famous Dionne Quintuplets, the first quintuplets to survive infancy, shown learning how to use a tyre pump before taking turns to ride their bicycle, circa 1943.

54 Bike lock

Mankind has sought to protect what it values since ancient times, as evidenced by the earliest examples of wooden locks dating back 6000 years that were found in Egyptian pyramids.

It is thought that the first metal – usually iron – locks and keys were invented by the Romans during the 1st millennia BC. The earliest bike locks – a length of stout chain secured with a metal padlock – date from the days of the first vélocipèdes and were found wherever there were bicycles. Exactly where and how bikes were secured, however, varied by country, with American locks being placed around the forks and the spokes, or connected to the pedal crank to the bicycle frame, whereas German steel locks of the early 20th century locked the rear wheel to the seat post.

By the 1920s, German companies Damm & La and GALVANOS were producing pressed-steel locks for the rear wheel. In Sweden, Optimus manufactured their first rear-wheel locks in the 1930s. These early O-locks worked by being fixed around the wheel to prevent riding, although they did not secure the frame to a stationary object and were easy to break open using a hammer. Despite their inherent weakness – the fact that a modern O-lock leaves the frame unsecured so a thief can simply carry the bike away – O-locks are still in use.

The challenge for bicycle-lock designers has been to secure both the wheels and the frame – particularly if a bike is fitted with a quick-release mechanism – while making their mechanisms as theft-proof as possible, something that neither D-locks nor cable locks have really achieved since both have both proved vulnerable to bicycle thieves armed with sturdy bolt cutters or jacks.

One of the most effective solutions is the Kryptonite lock, an amended D-lock design, developed in the USA in the 1970s, which was designed with a flat steel shackle, crossbar and steel sleeve to make the padlock mechanism resistant to bolt cutters.

With nearly 400,000 bikes stolen in Britain every year – that's about one bike every 90 seconds – it makes sense to invest in some kind of security device for your much-prized bicycle, especially since only an estimated 5 per cent of household contents insurance policies cover the cost of a replacement. It is worth investing, therefore, in a solid lock, preferably one carrying the gold 'Sold Secure' rating, an independent safety certification scheme which rates bike locks as bronze, silver or gold. There are plenty of designs to choose from: the wheel has now turned full circle with improved cable locks, based on the earliest chain locks, joining D-locks such as the Kryptonite in popularity. Modern bikes may also come fitted with GPS tracking systems for extra security, and better safety accreditation through the independent Sold Secure scheme, gives cyclists peace of mind when choosing how best to protect their precious – and often costly – machines.

Whether chain or U-shaped, a good lock is essential piece of equipment for every cyclist, as this broken bicycle with its front tyre missing, tied to a stand on a street in New York demonstrates!

55 Panniers

The gentle pastime of cyclotourism would be impossible without the invention of the pannier bag.

As transportation migrated from horse to wheel, so too did the means of carrying essential items of kit. For centuries, horses had transported goods in saddlebags and box-shaped panniers and these proved a perfect fit for the bicycle, something that designers and manufacturers were quick to realise.

In 1884, American John B. Wood was the first to take out a patent for his 'saddle bag for bicycles' – essentially a pair of hinged leather briefcases to be carried over the back wheel – but there were several other types available around the world. Of these, names of note included British firms Carradice and Brooks (the latter being best known for their leather saddles (*see* pp. 48–49), both of which produced saddlebags and panniers in the UK in the 1930s. Of particular importance was the treated cotton duck – a heavy woven cotton canvas fabric – that Carradice pioneered. This had distinct advantages over leather, being less prone to abrasions, as well as being waterproof.

Whatever the fabric, these types of transverse saddlebags, held under the rear of the saddle and often featuring pockets for essentials such as tools and snacks, were particularly popular in the UK and remain so for riders commuting to work.

Larger panniers, however, were more often to be seen in France, where Paul de Vivie had popularised cyclotourism – cycling purely for pleasure – in Europe in the 1890s, having himself been inspired by the founding in 1878 of the UK's Bicycle Touring Club (later the Cyclists' Touring Club and now called Cycling UK, the oldest touring club in the world). Vivie executed a series of long-distance rides that observed his seven commandments of cyclotouring (these included taking short breaks, never pushing oneself to exhaustion, and eliminating the use of tobacco and alcohol) and discovered that box-shaped panniers slung over the back wheel proved to be the perfect means of transporting a cyclotourist's essential equipment.

In fact, panniers had first featured on the Draisine, where they were front-mounted, made of leather and smaller than the rear-mounted variety. However, the longer sightseeing excursions that Vivie advocated required something more substantial and waterproof. The first real modern panniers – hardwearing and rigid – were patented in the 1970s as 'a pair of stiff-backed compartmentalized fabric bags' suitable for mounting over the rear wheel. These are also ideal for commuters who need to carry a change of clothes to the office.

Touring bikes are distinctive to look at, since they feature steel frames, comfortable saddles, sturdy mudguards and those all-important panniers – quite different from road-racing bikes or mountain bikes. Today's cyclotourists are likely to also be equipped with sophisticated equipment such as GPS and weather-resistant, easily detachable panniers suitable for transportation by aeroplane. Touring with a bicycle remains commonplace in Europe, the UK and the USA, and the rise in popularity of cycling means that there are now few places on the globe where a cyclotourist can't simply strap on their panniers, fix their eyes on the distant road and ride.

A cyclist in Holland transports a dog in one of the panniers on the back of her bicycle, circa 1954. The invention of the pannier helped make cyclotourism possible, allowing cyclists to carry their essential kit with them.

Mudguards

For the serious amateur cyclist, mudguards (called fenders in the USA) are an absolute necessity. Exactly as their name suggests, they stop mud and other detritus from flicking off the road surface on to your clothes – and, more importantly, your bike. Britain's Beryl Burton, perhaps the greatest woman cyclist of all time, swore by them. 'Except for racing,' she wrote, 'I can see no excuse for subjecting your body and bicycle to wheel spray on wet roads.'

If keeping clean is your goal, then touring and 'Dutch'-style bikes are most suitable, since they usually feature an ample mudguard. The latter kind – built for comfort, not speed – is derived from the safety bike, and retains many of the features popular on women's bikes of the 1890s, including mudguards to stop a lady's skirts from getting caked in filth. Indeed, advertising for the first safety bicycles made much of the fact that its riders could include a conservatively dressed lady or gentleman, pedalling along in an upright position, their attire kept pretty much pristine.

In response to the public desire for clean, comfortable bikes during a time when leisure cyclists rode around town in their ordinary clothes, the world's oldest bicycle manufacturer, Bianchi, produced a particularly stylish model throughout the early part of the 20th century, featuring a crossbar and a full set of mudguards. Despite what you might think, these mudguards could look classy, as was demonstrated by Claud Butler's 1937 Tour d'Angleterre bicycle, whose racy lines and drop handlebars were not marred by its slimline fenders. In fact, mudguards attained a certain element of cool when they started to appear on classic children's bicycles such as the Schwinn Sting-Ray and the Raleigh Chopper in the 1960s and 1970s, although for adult bikes, mudguards have always been strictly utilitarian.

The use of an accessory such as the mudguard, then, marked a clear distinction between cycling as an active sport with clear competitive goals and cycling as a leisure pursuit, where obvious displays of exertion were entirely beside the point. These curved arches of metal bolted to the frame are thus a symbol of the demarcation between the elite and the utilitarian cyclist. Despite this, many competitive cyclists are of the same opinion as ex-professional rider Michael Barry, who wrote on the website *Competitive Cyclist* in 2013 of his old Bianchi city bike: 'the race bikes I've ridden over the years were tools to get a job done, while the city bikes are a part of me, or, perhaps, I am a part of them.'

Modern mudguards may clip to the frame, roll up when not in use or be manufactured from recycled plastic. Despite these advances, however, there remains something romantic about the city or touring bike with its sturdy frame and that most practical of accessories, the mudguard, speaking as it does of a gentler time before the rise of MAMIL (Middle-Aged Man in Lycra) and the new elitism of the newbie with his high-performance bike.

Multiple world and British champion Beryl Burton, shown here with her daughter Denise, swore by mudguards for winter training. In the World Championships between 1959 and 1967, BB as she was known, won seven gold, four silver and three bronze medals. Mother and daughter raced together in the 1972 World Championships.

57 Puncture-repair kit

The John Bull puncture-repair kit evokes sighs of nostalgia from English-speaking cyclists, but it was a Frenchman, Louis Rustin, who first came up with the idea of repairing punctured inner tubes using an economic rubber patch in the early 1920s.

In 1903, the roads of France might have been thronged with bicycles but equally numerous were the number of punctures a rider might expect. Repairs could take a great deal of time, involving a trip to the local bike shop to separate the tyre from the rim (these were often glued together), a situation that the young French cyclist was determined to remedy with a swift, practical and economic solution. Thus *La Rustine* was born.

Though he was the owner of a Parisian bicycle-repair shop, Louis Rustin was also an amateur racing cyclist and knew from bitter experience how costly a puncture could be. Working with his friend Paul Doumenjou, a chemical engineer, Rustin came up with a solution for the still relatively new pneumatic tyre, going on in 1908 to patent a 'device to avoid bursting tires for all vehicles' consisting of a leather strip designed to be glued inside the tube of the tyre to strengthen it.

But Rustin still wasn't satisfied, and carried on working away at the problem for more than a decade until 1921, when he finally came up with and patented the Rustine – a small rubber patch that could be glued to the tyre for a quick and easy repair. At that time, Rustin sponsored one of the great French stars of the age, André Leducq, and word of the new puncture-repair kit rapidly

spread through the peloton, no doubt helped by the clever and creative marketing strategy of filling seats at track events with young cyclists who would call out '*Rustines! Rustines!*' whenever a rider got a puncture. Indeed, so highly esteemed was the kit and its inventor that his name entered cycling parlance, with The Rustine Trophy being awarded at the Tour de France and the *Kilometre Rustine* becoming hotly contested on the track. With its distinctive red-and-white tins, the Rustine brand became as recognisable a French marque as Michelin. When a popular French chanteur performed '*La Mome Rustine*' ('The Rustine Kid') in 1955, the product's place in French commercial and cultural life was assured.

Similar kits produced by John Bull in the UK were also part of the cultural landscape, especially for children. Anyone with a bicycle knew how to rough up the rubber around the puncture with the small piece of sandpaper provided, then apply glue to the rubber patch before smoothing it over the hole. As a bonus, the kits would also work with a punctured football.

Although John Bull kits have not been made since 1976, the Rustine factory is still very much in operation and in 2011 the company brought back its famous trophy to be awarded to the most stylish rider at The Retro 1903 *sportive* in Angers. Sponsored events and trophies aside, however, it is for the invention of those little rubber patches in their bright-red tin that Louis Rustin has earned the gratitude of cyclists everywhere.

Whether Rustines or John Bull,
every keen cyclist of a certain age
knows how to mend a puncture
with a little rubber patch.

Global Positioning System (GPS) was developed by the US Military at the height of the Cold War, but this extraordinary technology can now be harnessed by anyone with a smartphone.

In 1957, scientists at the Massachusetts Institute of Technology (MIT) noticed that the radio signals from the newly launched Soviet Sputnik satellite were stronger as they approached the Earth and fainter as it moved away. This simple observation was the catalyst for what would become known as GPS, which is based on the theory that satellites can be tracked from Earth by registering the strength of their radio signals, and receivers can be tracked by their distance from the satellite. Numbers have risen from the original five satellites of the US Navy TRANSIT system – developed to locate submarines – to the 30 satellites that today make up the GPS constellation translating time and geographically stamped data to receivers around the world.

Smartphone apps harnessing the power of GPS have multiplied since its licence for civilian use was approved in 2000. Satellite navigation (satnav) is popular with cyclotourists for planning and recording their travels, and for professional cycling teams there are huge advantages to being able to track a rider's position, effort and power output during a race, allowing team managers to refine tactics and training. Moreover, both teams and race coverage can now pinpoint time gaps with great accuracy.

GPS use has trickled down to amateur cyclists, too, and there is no app more popular with professionals and amateurs alike than Strava. Originally mooted in 1996 as a way for college friends to virtually train together, the original app was developed in 2009 to tie in with the popularity of Garmin GPS devices for athletes.

The name 'Strava' comes from the Swedish word 'to strive'. After recording your activity – cycling and running remain the most popular – on a compatible GPS device, a user uploads the data to Strava and can then analyse and compare data with friends and professionals. These Strava 'segments', as they're known, have become fiercely competitive – none more so than the Strava King/Queen of the Mountains (KOM/QOM).

It's quite simple. Ride as hard as you can up the climb of your choice and upload your data. Then compare this with the times of other riders, amateur and professional, from across the world. Strava has now also added the ability to visualise a user's yearly statistics in video form. In 2015 alone, 5.3 bike rides were logged every second – that's an astonishing 4.5 billion kilometres (2.8 billion miles) of riding logged on the site.

However, Strava isn't all about owning a particular climb. Users have worked out complicated routes that produce Strava art – everything from bicycles and Thanksgiving turkeys to marriage proposals.

Thirty satellites currently make up the GPS
constellation. Once the preserve of the US military,
global positioning can now be accessed by anyone with
a smartphone or a GPS device. Here are two examples of
Strava art by David Taylor: 'Big Bike' and 'Pony Ride'.

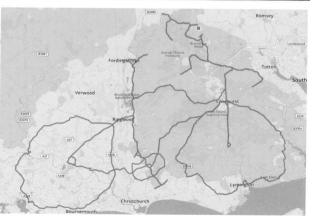

59 GoPro camera

The first attempts to capture action footage from sporting events were made in the 1960s, when athletes wore helmet-mounted cameras to capture their exploits. Since then, action cameras have become a multibillion industry thanks to one innovation: the GoPro.

GoPro was not, however, the first action camera – that title belongs to the space cameras developed by camera company Hasselblad and NASA in 1963 and used in the moon landings later that decade. Back on Earth a few years later, Steve McQueen wore a camera taped to his helmet during the filming of *Le Mans* in 1971 to provide 'point of view' footage during the action sequences.

Although the footage McQueen captured was acceptable, this and other cameras that were strapped to helmets at that time were comparatively large, heavy and robust, meaning they were uncomfortable, unaerodynamic and added to a rider's overall weight. It wasn't until 1986 that the Canon Ci-10 – a pocket camera weighing less than 300g (10½oz) – paved the way for the development of a real action camera when it was used to produce the first POV footage transmitted from the USGP 500 motorcycle World Championship. Helmet cams, the size and shape of a lipstick and worn above the ear, were introduced in American football in 1991, but cost an eye-watering US$20,000 per unit, so the idea of an action camera for large numbers of cyclists remained unviable.

And then came the GoPro, invented by a young entrepreneur and adrenaline junkie called Nick Woodman, who managed to capture images of himself surfing in Australia using a 35mm camera strapped to his hand with an elastic band. Woodman went on to develop the first GoPro prototype in 2004 – a small, rugged and waterproof camera designed to capture surfers in action. Though analogue and unable to record video, it was easy to use and accessible to all, since the wrist mount fitted a wide range of ages. Moreover, it was affordable: that first GoPro HERO cost just US$20.

Since Woodman sold his first GoPros live on air on shopping channel QVC in 2005, his product has developed exponentially. Now offering high-definition video, GoPro is the fastest-growing camera company in the USA and has made its founder a multibillionaire, though money wasn't its inventor's original motivation, as Woodman says: 'Our goal was to create a celebration of inspired humans doing rad stuff around the world.' This it most certainly has done, giving every weekend warrior the opportunity to star in his or her own action video.

The applications for cycling are obvious. GoPro now partners with ASO, owners of the Tour de France, to provide online footage directly from riders during the race. French rider Jérémy Roy regularly releases his own video footage of events in the peloton, enriching the spectator-viewing experience, and GoPro footage is another weapon in the arsenal of team managers looking for a tactical advantage.

Elsewhere, GoPro is also popular with amateur cyclists and commuters for one very important reason: safety. Increasingly, riders are using helmet cams to document and report instances of road rage and reckless driving and as a deterrent to dangerous drivers; digital footage is admissible in court in the UK and USA, though across many European countries strict liability laws mean a driver is automatically at fault anyway, rendering such evidence unnecessary. Moreover, wearing a GoPro may also make its user themselves more safety conscious and observant of the laws of the road, restoring some credibility to the battered image of so-called 'Lycra louts' everywhere.

Nick Woodman, founder and Chief Executive Officer of GoPro, shown holding one of early models of the GoPro Hero 3+ camera. GoPro partners with ASO to produce footage from inside the Tour de France and is popular with amateur riders as a safety measure.

60 Bicycle-powered washing machine

The internet is littered with plans for how to build your own bicycle-powered washing machine, but Alex Gadsden actually put his plans into action and in 2006 built the Cyclean, a machine that washes and spins your laundry using pedal power alone. Since then, students in China have gone one step further and designed an exercise bike with a washer drum integrated into its wheel. The applications of pedal-powered technology such as this for off-grid communities in the poorer parts of the world are exciting and possibly endless.

Of course, as with anything pedal-power related, it's all been done before; in the 1870s, pedals and cranks were being attached to tools such as lathes, saws and drills. Where previously hand cranks might have been utilised, pedal power allowed the leg muscles – the strongest in the body – to generate optimal power. The rise of the combustion engine and the ability to generate electricity put paid to pedal power, however, and by the start of World War I many of the pedal-powered machines had been melted down for use in the war effort.

There was a brief resurgence in interest in pedal power as a feasible alternative technology in the early 1970s during the first oil crisis, and companies researched and invested in the possibility of extending the use of pedal power to almost all machinery – even a bicycle-powered petrol (or gas) pump. As the crisis waned, so too did enthusiasm, until concerns about global warming in the 1990s brought renewed interest in the use of bicycles to generate electricity.

Throughout the developing world there has been a raft of projects that harness the power of the pedal to automate simple tasks. Take, for instance, the Dynapod – designed by British engineer Alex Weir in Africa in the 1970s – which is equipped with multiple drives to power a variety of different machinery; and the EnergyCycle, developed around the same time, which could be used to plough fields efficiently. Since then, there have been numerous pedal-powered innovations, including: Maya Pedal machines, which are used in Guatemala to power grinders, water pumps, nut-shellers, washing machines and blenders, the technology of which has evolved over time to include more sophisticated purpose-built units with a flywheel rather than just old bicycle parts; the VitaGoat Cycle Grinder, which is at the heart of a complete food-processing unit in developing countries in Asia and Africa; and the 'Made in Kenya' project, a concept conceived by two Swedish students for a pedal-powered juice press that, crucially, comes with pictogram instructions for its construction – think Ikea for farm machinery – rather than written ones, in order to overcome communication and illiteracy issues in rural areas.

In the developed world, companies are experimenting with cargo bikes for making deliveries, and there are multiple other pedal-powered devices, ranging from smoothie machines to lawnmowers. And it doesn't stop there. The interest in renewables and concerns about oil and the future of fossil fuels are driving new investigations into what pedal power can achieve. The day is perhaps coming when you will be able to hook up your home trainer and power your household appliances as you exercise.

The Cyclean Pedal-Powered Washing
Spin Dryer Machine, invented by
Alex Gadsden. One day all appliances
may be pedal powered.

61 MAMIL

Where once men of a certain age with a disposable income and a mid-life crisis on their hands would get a divorce and buy a sports car, they are now more likely to shave their legs, squeeze into Lycra shorts and spend thousands on a top-of-the-range road bike.

The term MAMIL – Middle Aged Men In Lycra – was coined by Michael Oliver in a Mintel market research report in 2010. Despite a 10 per cent fall in the number of bicycles sold in the UK, he noticed a 4 per cent rise in the total size of the bike market. So what was driving the growth? Answer: a new market segment of well-off men in their thirties and forties who shopped at the best supermarkets and read the better class of newspaper had swapped Ferraris for a Trek Madone or three. As Oliver noted in his report: 'Thirty or forty years ago, people would ride a bike for economic reasons, but our research suggests that nowadays a bicycle is more a lifestyle addition, a way of demonstrating how affluent you are.'

But what was really attracting these weekend warriors to a sport that had fallen out of favour in the UK? For the most part, it can be put down to one thing: there has been a change at the top of the leaderboard of world cycling. Cycling now has famous English-speaking heroes; no longer do the European nations dominate, as they had traditionally done since cycle racing was invented.

Since 2011, English-speaking riders have dominated the Tour de France, with Australia's Cadel Evans and Britons Sir Bradley Wiggins and Chris Froome winning five out of six races (up to 2016). Other high-profile riders include Britain's Mark Cavendish, who took the rainbow stripes in 2011, and the infamous Lance Armstrong who, though he may now languish in disgrace, his name removed from the record books, was undoubtedly once

immensely popular. His cancer survivor's story helping him to transcend the sport and become a global star, and the huge significance of the Livestrong yellow wristband cannot be understated.

Add in a plethora of world titles and gold medals on the track at the Olympics for Team GB and you have a newly 'cool' and successful sport a nation can get behind, often dubbed 'the new golf' for its popularity among businessmen and entrepreneurs.

Then there's the gadgetry and the endless opportunities for customisation of frames and components, which appeals to tech-heads and gadget-geeks. At the other end of the spectrum, cycling chimes with the way we live now, with its focus on health and well-being and having impeccable green credentials.

However, the picture isn't all rosy – and the MAMIL, with his fancy high-spec kit and competitive attitude, may even deter others from getting on their bikes. Another deterrent may be the injuries – cycling requires a high level of overall fitness, quick reflexes and great bike-handling skills and many jump in the saddle just as those physical abilities start to fade, resulting in accidents. One high-profile casualty, U2's Bono, for instance, required extensive surgery to his face and metal plates in his arm after an accident when riding in New York City.

Despite these drawbacks, the urge to squeeze into tight-fitting Lycra remains, and for this new breed of monied 'lifestyle' riders, UK cycling brand Rapha – with its stripped-back, retro aesthetic and one-time sponsorship of the MAMIL's favourite Team Sky – has become the kit of choice. But perhaps they would do well to remember Velominati Rule #17: 'Wearing Pro team kit is questionable if you're not paid to wear it.'

'Becoming a MAMIL' by Dave Walker, taken from *The Cycling Cartoonist*. Cycling is popular with middle aged men in Lycra everywhere.

BECOMING A MAMIL*

*MIDDLE-AGED MAN IN LYCRA

① BE A MAN

(YOU CAN MOST CERTAINLY BE A WOMAN OF COURSE. YOU WILL JUST NEED TO MAKE A MINOR ADJUSTMENT TO THE ACRONYM)

② REACH MIDDLE AGE

SOMEWHERE AROUND HERE

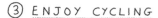

BIRTH   DEATH

③ ENJOY CYCLING

WOO HOO

④ REALISE THAT CYCLING SHORTS WOULD MAKE THE WHOLE EXPERIENCE FAR MORE COMFORTABLE

AREA OF PADDING

WOW. THIS MAKES SUCH A DIFFERENCE

⑤ LEARN THAT IT IS FAR MORE EFFICIENT TO USE SHOES THAT CLIP INTO THE PEDALS

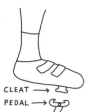

CLEAT →
PEDAL →

⑥ DECIDE THAT, HAVING GOT THE SHORTS, THE MATCHING JERSEY IS AN ENTIRELY SENSIBLE ADDITION

⑦ MAKE FRIENDS WITH STEVE, WHO HAS NUMEROUS BIKES, ALL MANNER OF KIT, EQUIPMENT, AND SUCHLIKE

STEVE'S SHED OF BICYCLE DELIGHTS

⑧ RESOLVE TO BE MORE LIKE STEVE

I'M GETTING NEW WHEELS

YES, I THINK I MIGHT GET NEW WHEELS TOO

⑨ YOU ARE MORE OR LESS THERE

62 Bloomers

The invention of the safety bicycle not only revolutionised personal transportation for women, it also prompted a radical reinvention of the conventional fashions of the day and the advent of 'bloomers' – loose, baggy trousers gathered in a cuff below the knee – which came to symbolise the newly liberated female, thanks to the woman they were named after, social reformer Amelia Bloomer.

Amelia Bloomer's garment was based on the kind of loose trousers traditionally worn by Turkish women. It was quickly taken up by members of the Rational Dress Society that formed in London in 1881 to promote practical dress for women, but was not widely adopted until the bicycle craze of the 1890s, when contemporary illustrations show young women cycling in practical bloomer costumes. So scandalous were these outfits considered at the time, however, that the Mayor of Chattanooga in the USA moved to ban them, declaring bloomers to be a 'menace to the peace and good morals of the male residents of the city', and many women refused to adopt them for fear of social approbation.

There were many strong practical reasons for dispensing with the heavy skirts and tight corsets that were the fashion, too. Despite the invention of the step-through frame in the 1880s to accommodate the voluminous dimensions of a full skirt, a gust of wind was enough to allow yards of fabric to become entangled in the bicycle chain. Dr Turner of the Cyclists' Touring Club recognised in 1900 that cycling in so-called 'rational dress' – usually a divided skirt over bloomers – was 'safer in that there is no skirt flapping about to get wound up in the machine.' Accidents on bicycles were common – in the 1891 *Sporting Life* one young woman recalled: 'skimming along like a bird, when there was an awful tug at my dress

and a cracking sound. Before I knew what was the matter I found myself lying on the road with the safety on top of me. My dress was so tightly wound around the crank bracket that I could not get up until I got free.'

The freedom of movement granted to women by the bicycle demanded that their dress be equally liberated. Choosing to ride a bike engaged women in a debate about femininity and appearance. One article on the 'New Woman' – made socially independent by her bicycle – noted that what society saw was not 'a new woman with bloomers, but a new edition of man.' This supposed masculinisation of women during the bicycle boom of the 1890s caused Dr J.B. Hawthorne, pastor of the First Baptist Church of Atlanta, to opine from the pulpit that women were 'riding to the devil in bloomers'.

Despite this censure, there was no stopping them. In 1885, 16-year-old Tessie Reynolds – clad in rational dress of a long jacket over knickerbockers that she described as being 'very comfortable and convenient' – covered the 120 miles from Brighton to London and back on a racing bike in a record time of 8 hours 38 minutes, including stops.

The same year, 25-year-old Annie Kopchovsky (or simply 'Londonderry', as she became known) pedalled into Boston, having completed the first-ever round-the-world trip by a woman. Leaving her three young children and setting off with little more than a pearl-handled revolver and a change of underwear, the diminutive Kopchovsky – who had barely learned to ride a bicycle – started her ride in a skirt and blouse, changed to bloomers during the journey, and finished in men's trousers. A firm believer in rational dress, she expressed the opinion that: 'in the near future all women, whether of high or low degree, will bestride the wheel, except possibly the narrow-minded, long-skirted, lean and lank element.'

An illustration of Amelia Bloomer (1818–1894), American feminist and champion of dress reform, wearing her new dress for women, known as 'bloomers'. These baggy garments were the forerunner of the rational cycling dress movement that revolutionised the way women dressed.

⬤63 Marriage certificate

When the safety bicycle detonated the cycling boom of the 1880s and 1890s it had one unexpected consequence that was so significant that it prompted biologist Steve Jones to rank the invention of the bicycle as the most important act in the history of mankind.

This was because, for the first time, men and women could extend the geographical area from which they could find a potential partner, and women in particular enjoyed a freedom hitherto unknown to them. The bicycle was no longer a rich man's plaything and the impact on female's emancipation was enormous. Women on bicycles became a common sight in public, prompting one journalist from the *American Sunday Herald* to declare in 1891: 'I had thought that cigarette smoking was the worst thing a woman could do, but I have changed my mind.' Freed of their corsets and their chaperones, women were able to venture further afield to see who caught their eye.

However, in 1896, the French actress Sarah Bernhardt was moved to opine sadly: 'The bicycle is on the way to transforming our way of life more deeply than you might think. All these young women and girls who are devouring space are refusing domestic family life.'

In 1895, the *New York World* even went so far as to publish a list of 41 'don'ts' for women on bicycles, including: 'don't wear a man's cap'; 'don't ask "what do you think of my bloomers?"'; 'don't go out after dark without a male escort'; and 'don't appear to be up on "records" or "record smashing." That is sporty.'

The naysayers were also concerned about the impact cycling would have on sexual propriety. Surely riding astride the new-fangled machine would habituate women to novel and unwelcome sexual stirrings? Would these 'new women' become both sexualised and masculinised by contact with their mechanical steeds? In response, so-called 'hygiene' saddles began to appear alongside raised handlebars to discourage the risk of women becoming over-stimulated by riding in the more aggressive style encouraged by drop handlebars.

However, popularity continued to rise. In 1895, 800,000 bicycles were manufactured in Britain. In 1896, the year of peak production, more than a million bicycles were made in the USA, and in Germany, 10% of women were riding bikes. The gender gap wasn't the only division being slowly but surely breached by the bicycle – the working classes, too, could now enjoy personal mobility, which had a huge social impact. In cities, tenements emptied and suburbs expanded to accommodate the new commuters.

Moreover, in countryside rural communities, where inbreeding was once a real problem that impacted upon public health, communities were widened and strengthened by the bicycle. In Britain alone, births registered during the period show surnames once confined to a small geographical area appearing many miles away from the communities with which they had long been associated.

An image of a wedding party on bicycles led by the bride and bridegroom, on the cover of a 1909 issue of *Le Petit Journal*, a Parisian newspaper published between 1863 and 1944. Biologist Steve Jones ranked the impact of the bicycle on the gene pool as one of the most significant events in human evolution.

MARIAGE EN BICYCLETTE

The bicycle may have emancipated some women in the 1890s but cycling remained a strongly gendered sport. Where manufacturers were happy to market the latest technological innovations in frames and wheels to their male clients, women's bicycles remained dainty, upright machines marketed for their elegance. For every 'Napoleon' bike there was a 'Josephine,' at least in the 1913 Sears catalogue.

The passion and enthusiasm for a 'life on the wheel' for females was communicated by word of mouth, and women shared their knowledge on everything from learning to ride a bicycle to what to wear and how to look after their machines. And they were evangelical about the benefits of cycling: 'it gives one the gratification of being one's own mistress' enthused one letter to the *New York Times* in 1896, 'there is the feeling of gratification in being independent from coachmen and grooms.'

Publishers were quick to notice this, and this colloquial knowledge was quickly codified in the form of cycling manuals by women, for women. These stood in stark contrast to other published information available at the time, which urged women to be upright and ladylike at all times. For instance, Maria Ward's *Bicycling for Ladies* (published in 1896) was an attempt to educate women in the 'laws of mechanics and of physiology that directly concern the cyclist'. In her chapter on 'Women and Tools' Ward writes: 'I hold that any woman who is able to use a needle or scissors can use other tools equally well. It is a very important matter for a bicyclist to be acquainted with all parts of the bicycle, their uses and adjustment.

Many a weary hour would be spared were a little proper attention given at the right time to your machine.'

Ward makes clear in the preface to her manual that in addition to imparting knowledge and advice, she has another mission: to combat the censure that women often met when riding their machines. The bicycle, she claimed, is a tool for self-determination: 'You have conquered a new world,' she writes, 'and exultingly you take possession of it.' Yet the book does make one concession to the mores of the time – the illustrations, based on Alice Austen's photographs of a rather grim-faced female rider, had been 'prettified' by the time they got to print.

Another publication by and for women was Frances Willard's 1895 manual *A Wheel Within a Wheel: How I Learned to Ride the Bicycle*, in which Willard details her attempts, at the age of 53, to accomplish a life on two wheels. Willard's eventual mastery of 'Gladys' is the tale of a thoroughly modern woman helping other women to access their 'natural love of adventure – a love long hampered and impeded.' This could be achieved, she wrote, by 'acquiring this new instrument of power and literally putting it underfoot.' It took Willard three months to finally ride off alone on 'the most remarkable, ingenious and inspiring motor ever yet devised on this planet.' Any failures on her part she put down to a 'wobbling will, not a wobbling wheel.'

Thanks to the efforts of Willard and Ward and their like, millions of women were now equipped to master their own destinies on two wheels. A few years later, they would take that same spirit on to the roads and into the skies.

An extract of *A Wheel Within A Wheel: How I Learned To Ride The Bicycle, With Some Reflections By The Way* showing a photograph of the author, the indomitable Frances Elizabeth Willard, published in 1895. Willard was 53 when she learned to ride a bike which she called Gladys.

Frances E Willard

A WHEEL WITHIN A WHEEL

HOW I LEARNED TO
RIDE THE BICYCLE

WITH SOME REFLECTIONS BY THE WAY

BY
FRANCES E. WILLARD

𝕴llustrated

FLEMING H. REVELL COMPANY
NEW YORK   CHICAGO   TORONTO
1895

Cycling For Kids

65 Stabilisers and the balance bike

Although the first bikes designed and built for children were introduced in 1910, they failed to catch on until the 1940s when American company Huffy introduced the 'Convertible'. With its bolt-on training wheels the Convertible revolutionised the market for children's bicycles; for the first time, you could learn to ride a bike without the need to concentrate on pedalling and balance at the same time. Stabilisers helped entire generations of children to become mobile and independent on two wheels before pedal-less balance bikes stole the show.

There are two inherent issues with learning to ride a bike. One is pedalling, and that's the problem that training wheels or stabilisers address. But the more difficult trick lies in persuading children that climbing aboard something as unstable as a bicycle won't necessarily result in tears and scraped knees. As Archibald Sharp wrote in his seminal book *Bicycles & Tricycles* in 1896: 'If the bicycle and rider be at rest, the position is thus one of unstable equilibrium, and no amount of gymnastic dexterity will enable the position to be maintained for more than a few seconds.'

Balance bikes – as their name suggests – solve the balance problem first. A pint-size, kid-friendly version of the Draisine, balance bikes have soared in popularity since the 2000s, with the US Strider brand recording sales of over 1 million bikes in the years since their launch in 2007. However, they're not cheap – the average balance bike costs twice as much as a conventional children's bike. So why choose a costly balance bike over a cheaper bike with training wheels? First, the perception is that the robust little wooden- or steel-framed bikes are

built to last, and can be handed down to younger siblings. Second, like the Draisine, they are propelled by pushing off against the ground and help children to master the tricky issue of equilibrium before they have to think about pedalling.

In 1997, when Rolf Mertens – an industrial designer and keen woodworker – decided to build his two-year-old son Niklas a bike without pedals from scratch, he took his cues from his countryman Karl Drais. Like the Draisine, the original LIKEaBIKE was made of wood. And like the Draisine, it caused gasps of amazement when Niklas first took it out for a spin. 'He got on and took off. He only stopped for meals and sleep,' said his mother Beate.

Like the bicycles of the 1940s, modern balance bikes often derive their design cues from cars, motorbikes and rockets. Easy to steer and relatively light to handle, they offer young riders a sense of stability and the opportunity to build leg strength ready for the challenge of turning pedals when they graduate to a proper bike. They also take away the drama and tears of transitioning from four wheels to two, and the uniquely adapted frame geometry helps to modify a child's stance on the bike to promote their all-important ability to balance. It should be noted, however, that a similar effect can be achieved by removing the pedals and dropping the seat and handlebars on a standard children's bike.

Whether you choose a balance bike or stabilisers, there is no doubt that getting children out and about exercising in the fresh air is beneficial, especially in light of the rise in sedentary screen-based activities and the growing problem of childhood obesity.

Stabilisers or no stabilisers? Thousands
of children have learned to ride with
training wheels or on the modern balance
bike – which allow children to get their
balance and make pedalling a breeze.

66 Raleigh Chopper

Throughout the 1970s, there was one present that most British children were desperate to receive for Christmas or birthdays: the Raleigh Chopper, a bicycle that still enjoys cult status today.

First marketed in 1969, the Raleigh Chopper – with its 'Easy Rider'-style handlebars, centrally mounted gear stick and banana saddle – weighed in at a hefty 18.5kg (40.8lb) and the first editions in 1969 cost a whopping £32 brand new (the equivalent of around £800 today).

Originally sketched on the back of an envelope by designer Alan Oakley, the Mark 1 took its design cues from the Schwinn Sting-Ray and, featuring chunky tyres and a kickstand, resembled a motorbike more than a standard bicycle. It became an instant classic – and instantly desirable.

The Mark 2, manufactured from 1972 to 1981, offered such modifications as a five-speed derailleur. Safety improvements were also made to the original design: the seat was moved forwards to prevent the front of the bicycle tipping up, and the handlebars were welded so they could no longer be pulled backwards. The unintended consequence was that the Mark 2 became virtually unsteerable and, although millions of Choppers graced roads and pavements worldwide, by the early 1980s the limelight was to be stolen by the new bike on the block: the low-profile BMX, which sounded the death knell for the iconic Chopper.

Despite this, for many the Chopper retained its appeal and they remain highly collectable. To this day, there exists a Raleigh Chopper Owners Club that sees 3000 enthusiasts congregate annually in Nottingham, England to celebrate all things Chopper. Extremely customisable, there were hundreds of different options for gearing and handlebars, so there is plenty for Chopper-geeks to choose from. The ultimate collectible, however, is the Silver Jubilee edition, released for Christmas 1976, of which only 768 were made.

Having been out of production for 21 years, the Chopper was relaunched in 2004 when Raleigh unleashed the Mark 3. This featured several major modifications, mostly to comply with new health and safety regulations: gone is the crotch-snagging central-mounted gear lever – replaced instead by a commemorative sticker; the seat has been redesigned to discourage pillion passengers; and that hefty steel frame has been replaced by one welded from aluminium-alloy tubing. However, the original anomaly of a 50cm (20in) back wheel and a 40cm (16in) front wheel remains, and it is instantly recognisable as being related to that must-have British biking icon of '70s schoolchildren.

No 1970s childhood was complete without a Raleigh
Chopper. The high raised handlebars, dual seat saddle,
and a central gear-change lever made the design an
instant classic. Intended to appeal to boys and girls from
8 to 14 years of age, it became an immediate success.

BMX

With its distinctive low-slung frame, 50cm (20in) wheels and high handlebars, the BMX (Bicycle Motorcross Bike) is popular with kids, racers and hipsters alike.

This history of the BMX starts with the Schwinn Sting-Ray. First produced in 1963, the 50cm (20in) wheeled bike with its short wheelbase and unique steering geometry is the blueprint for the modern BMX bike. It handled well but, most importantly, it was ideal for doing tricks and stunts, pulling a wheelie and riding dirt trails. By 1968, an estimated 70 per cent of all bikes sold in the USA were Sting-Rays, or copies of Sting-Rays, and its huge success inspired the Raleigh Chopper in the UK.

The next step in the evolution of the BMX occurred when Bruce Brown released his motorbike film *On Any Sunday* in 1971, during which he featured a few minutes' footage of kids on Sting-Rays modified to look like motorcross bikes riding across a dirt field in Southern California. This proved to be the spark that lit the fire under the BMX craze of the 1970s and saw BMX tracks mushroom across the USA.

The original BMX tracks featured a steep hill start and a series of obstacles, including jumps and rollers, on a winding track. There were categories for under and over 13s, generally riding standard street bikes and wearing jeans, T-shirts and a helmet. It was zany, occasionally dangerous and utterly addictive. By 1977, the American Bicycle Association (ABA) had formed to codify the rules of the fledgling sport, and 34 years later, in 2011, the ABA purchased the assets of its struggling rival, the National Bicycle League, and rebranded as BMX USA to encompass the BMX disciplines: BMX racing and BMX freestyle, the latter of which was developed in 1979 to enable riders to concentrate on performing astonishing tricks and jumps on their tough little machines.

Spotting the connection with motocross, Yamaha was quick to develop the monoshock Moto-Bike, and they were not alone in jumping on the bandwagon; other racers began modifying their Sting-Rays, and Speedway motorbike-builders Redland developed the first tubular BMX forks in 1974. The change of pace was intense, the challenge for designers being to produce a lightweight machine that was fast and manoeuvrable yet capable of producing huge airs and withstanding brutal shocks. They were mostly successful, and the 12.2kg (27lb) Mongoose Supergoose, with its steel stems and cranks, knobby tyres and moulded plastic seat, in particular, was hugely popular in the 1980s.

Since then, designers have continued to modify and improve upon earlier designs, and a modern BMX bike such as the Ripper X weighs in at under 9kg (20lb) and features alloy wheels and an aluminium frame. Moreover, so successful were many of the modifications made by BMX innovators – such as the use of chrome-moly frames – that they crossed over into another fledgling sport, mountain biking.

BMX today features supersized versions of the old rollers and berms, and was part of the first X Games in 1995. It later achieved Olympic recognition as part of the 2008 Beijing Olympics, with gold medals going to Māris Štrombergs for Latvia in the men's event and Anne-Caroline Chausson for France in the women's.

Durable and easy to handle, the BMX makes an ideal first bike for an older child, and it's fair to say that many a lifelong love affair with cycling has started on their 50cm (20in) wheels.

Young BMX racer Betsy Edmunson stands with her BMX bike in 1992. The low-slung stunt bike with its 20 inch wheels was inspired by the phenomenally popular Schwinn Sting-Ray of the 1960s. Easy to handle and ideally suited to the rough and tumble of BMX, the BMX bike is loved by kids, racers and hipsters alike.

It's a common sight on the streets of the Netherlands – a parent carrying their baby, often in an adapted car seat, on their bike. Almost from birth, Dutch children are used to travelling everywhere by bicycle, either seated behind or in front of their parent, and the Dutch cargo bike or *bakfiets* – with its longer wheelbase – is particularly well adapted to taking a young passenger.

However, the idea of taking your child along for a ride stretches right back to the birth of the bicycle, when a few Draisine riders would pass a strap around themselves and their child and place the child's feet into specially adapted panniers. This was not, however, a common sight, and it wasn't until the evolution of the safety bicycle that young passengers became more commonplace.

The geometry of the Rover was particularly suitable for the addition of an extra saddle on the top tube, so that the child sat cradled in the adult's arms. Charles Harvey of Philadelphia filed his patent for a child seat that enabled this in 1889 and, with the addition of a footrest bolted to the down tube, this became popular in Britain and elsewhere during the 1890s. It was not the only type on the market, however, and rival products included a front-mounted child seat composed of a steel framework housing a wicker shell, which was patented in 1891 by British hotelier and bicycle manufacturer Dan Albone.

The seat continued to evolve, slowly, and in 1914, Adolf Lofman – a Berlin-based bicycle manufacturer – took the basic Albone design and produced front-, rear- and top tube-mounted versions. Further developments included the Rambler company's No 4 carrier of the 1930s, which could be adapted into a parcel carrier by removing the wicker basket, and the Bulldog child's seat, developed by August Maier in Germany in the 1940s, which took the form of a saddle-shaped seat that plugged easily in and out of a mount securely bolted on to the bicycle's top tube. This simple seat is still in production today.

Whatever its incarnation, the front-mounted seat remained popular up to the end of World War II for use with younger children (it proved unsuitable for older, heavier ones), and it has never gone out of fashion in the Netherlands, where babies are often carried in a car seat attached to a special mount on the handlebars.

By contrast, the rear-mounted child seat was slow to catch on, although it is now the most popular style of child carrier for older children, protecting them from flying debris and the impact of head-on collisions. The first ones appeared in 1936, when the GMG company in the Netherlands produced a rudimentary affair that featured a cushioned seat and back rest, with a safety strap around the chest and two metal pegs for the feet to rest on. By the 1940s, however, folding rear-mounted bicycle seats that doubled as luggage racks were in vogue and remained popular into the 1970s, when the general decline in cycling meant that the child seat fell out of use in many areas.

These days popularity is on the increase, with over 100,000 people in the UK regularly participating in Sky Ride Big Bike family events. In the Netherlands, where the commitment to building an exemplary network of cycle paths meant cycling was more popular than ever as an activity for all the family, and still is to this day. There, it is common to see modern rear-mounted seats, which are generally composed of a hard plastic shell incorporating leg protection, footrests and a safety harness, as well as bike trailers, which attach to the frame and are towed behind the bike.

A family of four out riding on a tandem bicycle with a child seat and a sidecar attached. The child seat or trailer is still an incredibly popular way to transport children in many countries.

69 Cycling Proficiency Test

Back in 1960s Britain, Lenny the Lion encouraged scores of schoolchildren to sign up for the test and thousands (including Prince Charles, who wobbled his way to a badge at Cheam School in 1960) responded.

The idea of a Cycling Proficiency Test in the UK was first proposed in the 1930s, but it wasn't until 1947 that a pilot scheme, involving seven children and run by the Royal Society for the Prevention of Accidents (RoSPA), was rolled out. In 1958, this became the government-backed National Cycling Proficiency Scheme, which was again rebranded, as Bikeability, in 2007. Administered by schools and local authorities, over the years the scheme has seen hundreds of thousands of children weave their way through traffic cones on their way to that much-cherished shiny badge, to be attached with pride to one's handlebars. Nowadays the badge is gone, replaced by a certificate, but the pride felt by those who have passed remains the same.

Cycling was once phenomenally popular in Britain: in 1949, journeys by bike accounted for one-third of the total distance travelled on British roads. Even in 1971, 75 per cent of junior-school children were cycling to school, a figure that had halved by 1990. Recent figures show that 90 per cent of British children have never cycled to school and, despite the best efforts of schemes such as the Cycling Proficiency Test, the number of children riding a bike has continued to fall as alternative wheeled forms of transport such as the scooter and the skateboard have risen in popularity. The picture is much the same in the USA, Canada and Australia, where cyclist-friendly policies and infrastructure are lacking and rates of children cycling also remain low.

By contrast, in the Netherlands, Germany and Denmark, cycling is fully integrated into everyday life. The extensive networks of bike paths mean that cyclists are not required to do battle with cars on the roads, with the result that 49 per cent of primary-aged children in the Netherlands cycle to school, as opposed to just 3 per cent of children in the UK. All Dutch children receive theory and practical cycle training as part of the school curriculum and driver training across Europe places special emphasis upon respecting other road users.

In response to the problem in Britain, Bikeability aims to give children the skills and confidence to tackle Britain's traffic-heavy roads. The potential benefits for children of regularly cycling are enormous: a bike is a clean, green method of transport offering a child greater independence and opportunities for outdoor exercise.

A school pupil in 1961 makes a right turn at a halt sign during a cycling proficiency test. The Cycling Proficiency Test and its successor, Bikeability, have taught thousands of children how to ride a bike safely.

Road Racing

The purpose of a leader's jersey is quite simple: its easily distinguishable block of colour amid the kaleidoscope of the peloton is a clear visual reminder of which cyclist is leading a race or one of the competitions within the race.

The most famous leader's jersey of them all is the Tour de France's *maillot jaune*, or yellow jersey. The biggest prize in cycling, the yellow jersey was also the first to have been presented to a rider and has a history dating back to 1919, when it went on the shoulders of Eugène Christophe. The idea itself (or so the official line goes; there is some debate about the matter) came from Alfred Baugé, a team director who had already experimented with cladding his soigneurs in yellow to make them more visible, who wondered if also getting the leading rider to wear the coloured jersey rather than just differently coloured epaulettes would distinguish him in the pack. It also so happened that *L'Auto*, the paper that had conceived and sponsored the race, was at the time printed on yellow paper. Thus the *maillot jaune* was born.

Or... at least this is the most plausible of the yellow-jersey creation myths, but there are others. These include the claim by three-times Tour winner Belgian Philippe Thys that he had been asked by Baugé to wear a yellow jersey as race leader in the 1913 race, and that a jersey had accordingly been purchased and presented. Another theory is that yellow was the only colour available for the special jersey in 1919, having fallen out of popularity during the war because of its association with cowardice. Whatever the truth, however, the colour was not popular, and Christophe said it made him feel like a canary.

Despite this, the yellow jersey stuck, with *L'Auto* editorialising that: 'our director has decided that the man at the head of the general classment of the race should wear a jersey in the colours of *L'Auto*.' In 1931, the Giro d'Italia followed suit, awarding a pink jersey, the *maglia rosa*, to the leader for the first time – the same colour as the pages of the *Gazzetta dello Sport* that owned the race.

A jersey to distinguish the leader on the points competition – points are awarded depending upon the order the cyclists place in intermediate sprints along the route or as they cross the finish line – was introduced in 1953. In the Tour de France, this is green, and in the Giro it's once again red – as it was when it was introduced in 1967 – though for most of its history it was a deep pinky-mauve and known as the *maglia ciclamino*.

Though the King of the Mountains distinction had been recognised in the Tour de France since the 1930s, the first official red-and-white polka-dot jersey (designed by the first sponsors, Poulain, to reflect the wrapper of one of their chocolate bars) wasn't awarded until 1975, the year the white jersey for the best young rider also appeared at the race. The Giro had also recognised the King of the Mountains in 1933 and had been slightly quicker to award him with a distinctive green jersey in 1974. Unlike the Tour, though, the Giro has often changed the colour of the lesser jerseys to reflect a change in sponsorship and this jersey is currently blue.

There have been other jerseys, too, including the now-defunct combined jersey of the Tour, which was a patchwork of the others and awarded to the most consistent rider overall; and the blue jersey that was awarded to the InterGiro leader. Other jerseys may appear in a cycling race – most notably the rainbow stripes of the world champion and national champion's jerseys – though the yellow and the pink remain the biggest prizes.

A painting of Eugène Christophe shown on the front cover of *La Vie au Grand Air*, an illustrated French sports magazine in publication between 1898 and 1922. Christophe was the first rider to wear the yellow jersey at the Tour de France, though he would never win the race overall.

Vie au Grand Air

Rainbow jersey

The first thing to note about the rainbow jersey, which the UCI awards to the best rider in their discipline decided in a single race at the World Championships on the track or the road, is that the colours aren't those of the traditional rainbow.

Instead, the stripes on the champion's jersey derive from the colours of the five Olympic rings (which stand for the five continents), and are displayed in the same order: blue, red, black, yellow and green on a plain white background. Now trademarked by the UCI, there are strict rules about who can and cannot don the rainbow jersey and when and where it should be worn. For instance, it must be worn in every competition the holder enters during the year of their reign, but only in the discipline in which it was won. So, for example, the world time-trial champion may only wear their jersey in time-trial events and stages, and the same rules apply to road-race world champions. At the end of the year, world champions are permitted to wear the rainbow stripes on their sleeve cuffs or collars for the rest of their careers.

The first World Championships were organised by the International Cycling Association that was in existence from 1892 until 1900, when they came under the auspices of the newly formed *Union Cycliste Internationale* (UCI). The first rainbow jersey was awarded for men at the 1927 World Championships at Nürburgring, Germany and for women in 1958 when the championships were held in Reims, France. It confers on its wearer a particular place of honour and respect in the peloton. This distinction is only surpassed by the yellow jersey that, should the world champion take the race lead, as Greg LeMond did in the 1990 Tour de France, takes precedence over the rainbow one.

Despite its undoubted prestige, there is a so-called 'curse of the rainbow jersey' based on the fact that many wearers have suffered incredible bad luck the year after they receive it. These include Tom Simpson, who became the first-ever British world champion in 1965, only to miss out on nearly all of the next season after breaking his leg skiing; Belgian Freddy Maertens, the 1981 winner, who won no races the following year and only two more in his entire career; and Ireland's Stephen Roche, the only rider besides Eddy Merckx to win the Giro, Tour and Worlds in the same season in 1987, who missed most of 1988 with a knee injury.

However, for every 'cursed' rider there has been another who has worn the rainbow jersey to great effect. Louison Bobet, for instance, the French rider who was the first to win three Tours de France in a row, won in 1955 as world champion. Four riders have won Milan–San Remo in the jersey and Poland's Michał Kwiatkowski, the 2014 champion, won the 50th edition of Amstel Gold in his rainbow stripes. As for Eddy Merckx, he won Paris–Roubaix, the Tour of Flanders, Milan–San Remo, the Tour of Lombardy and Liège–Bastogne–Liège resplendent in the rainbow bands of world champion.

Tom Simpson became the first ever British World Road Race champion in 1965, winning the coveted rainbow striped jersey. He is shown below wearing the rainbow jersey before the first stage of the 1966 Tour de France.

Domestique/*gregario*

The humble domestique (or his Italian counterpart the *gregario*) is a rider who rarely seeks individual glory, instead putting himself entirely at the service of his team leader.

The term 'domestique' was first used derogatively by Henri Desgrange to describe a cyclist he suspected of riding in the service of another for financial gain. Riders were already seen as workmen rather than sportsmen, and were known colloquially as *ouvriers de la pedale*, or pedal workers. Desgrange was deeply opposed to collaboration between cyclists, even though the domestique who rode to protect his leader had been around for some time.

The role of the domestique was not to win, but to help his leader to win, as described by one of Gino Bartali's *gregari*: 'the kilometres I rode were not for me, they were for Bartali.' And such is the domestique's lot – to ride for kilometre after kilometre taking the full force of the wind to protect their leader, and to fetch and carry without ever seeking glory for themselves. Journalist Jean-Luc Gatellier, wrote of one of Fausto Coppi's most faithful helpers, Andrea Carrea: 'he was a *gregario* par excellence, he refused the slightest bit of personal glory.'

Sometimes, however, the domestiques did triumph. There is a well-known tale of how the same *gregario*, Andrea Carrea, joined a breakaway move during the Tour de France purely to protect his leader's interests and in so doing, entirely unwittingly rode himself into the yellow jersey. The Italian was beside himself. What would Coppi think? When his leader came to congratulate him, Carrea burst into tears, crying: 'You must understand that I did not want this jersey, Fausto. I have no right to it. A poor man like me, the yellow jersey?' Of such stuff is a true *gregario* made.

Coppi himself had also once been a *gregario* himself, riding in the service of legendary cyclist Gino Bartali, and he is not the only great rider who has fulfilled this role before going on to achieve personal glory: three-times Tour de France winner Greg LeMond started his career in the service of five-times winner Bernard Hinault; and Chris Froome – the first Briton to win the yellow jersey twice – rose in prominence as a domestique for Sir Bradley Wiggins. Which just goes to show that even great champions can start their life as humble domestiques, perhaps because, as Charly Wegelius explains in his book *Domestique*: 'the key thing I had to learn was that a domestique has to be almost as strong as his leader, and he must also be smart and aware of what he is doing.'

With the advent of two-way radio communication, the situation has changed somewhat and modern domestiques are shuffled around the peloton like pawns as their directors communicate the ever-changing tactics through their earpieces. This shift towards others doing the thinking for the riders is neatly summed up by Sean Yates, voted one of the 10 greatest domestiques ever (the very best earn themselves the ranking of *superdomestique* or *gregario-de-luxe*), who said of his job: 'Cycling's the easiest thing to do in the world, aside from the physical side. Of course you suffer some days but you're told where to go and when – it's straightforward.'

Greg LeMond and Bernard Hinault shown during a rest day of the 1985 Tour de France. Although LeMond rode as Hinault's domestique in 1985, he won the race outright the following year.

73 *Lanterne rouge*

The existence of the term *lanterne rouge* – the rider who finishes last on the general classification of the Tour de France – proves that sometimes the last can be first when it comes to publicity.

The nickname *lanterne rouge* comes from the red lantern that would be hung from the last carriage of a train around the turn of the 19th century to clearly show where the back of the locomotive lay, and was adopted by cycling as the name for the last-placed rider.

The very first *lanterne rouge* in cycling terms was 36-year-old Arsène Millocheau, who finished the 1903 Tour de France 64 hours 57 minutes and 8 seconds behind the winner, Maurice Garin, a time gap that remains the widest margin between the winner and the last-placed man in the history of the Tour. Millocheau, something of a veteran, had ridden the first Paris–Brest–Paris in 1891, and, seemingly undeterred by his lack of success in the 1903 Tour, went on to tackle the Paris–Brest–Paris race again in 1921 at the age of 54. Evidently a real lover of all things to do with bicycles, he later opened a bike shop in Paris and worked there until his death at the age of 81.

The term originates from, and is most closely associated with, the Tour de France. Many cyclists have borne the title; in each race only a handful of riders are capable of taking the biggest prize, while any one of a hundred or so can have the dubious honour of taking the *lanterne rouge*. There is no official sponsorship or prize money associated with last place, yet for fans the *lanterne rouge* remains one of the most romantic figures in the sport – the rider who hung on with grim determination to make it all the way to Paris without falling by the wayside.

Moreover, in the 1950s, when the lucrative post-Tour criterium circuit began to take off, being the *lanterne rouge* meant guaranteed invites, something that wasn't to be sniffed at in the days before million-dollar or -euro salaries. History is therefore peppered with tales of cyclists deliberately riding to be tail-end Charlies, or climbing off their bikes and hiding until they were certain they would be the last rider across the line. Notorious among these talented shirkers was the Belgian Edwig Van Hooydonck – the last-placed finisher in the 1993 Tour – a rider who was perfectly capable of doing well in the Tour since he had won the one-day classic, the Tour of Flanders, not once but twice.

In Italy, the Giro d'Italia also recognised the last-placed rider, awarding him the *maglia nera* (black jersey) between 1946 and 1951. The prize was withdrawn in 1951 after riders complained that too much attention was being given to the rider in last place. Indeed, the concept had been an instant hit with fans, who would hold up placards saying 'long live last place!' Moreover, some villages would even offer prize money and free board and lodgings to the black jersey-holder. Little wonder, then, that just as in the Tour, riders would work hard to keep hold of last place, often hiding in farms or enjoying leisurely lunches to do so. These included Luigi Malabrocca, twice winner of the coveted prize, who would go on to become world cyclocross champion, and Giovanni Pinarello, who enjoyed a lap of honour with the victor at the end of the 1921 race. The latter's pleasure at securing last place must have been fleeting, however, since he was dropped from his team – Bottecchia – the following year, though he did go on to found the iconic bicycling brand that still bears his name.

French cyclist Guy Million riding with the *lanterne rouge* during the 1957 Tour de France. The *lantern rouge* is the traditional symbol for the rider finishing last in the general classification of the Tour de France.

Podium

Honouring the winner of a cycling race is a tradition that has been around since James Moore won the first-ever long-distance bike race, Paris–Rouen, in the 1860s, and was handed a trophy by the mayor of Rouen. Forty years later, images of Maurice Garin, winner of the first Tour de France, show the diminutive Frenchman garlanded in flowers, draped in a tricolore sash and surrounded by stern-faced gentlemen in top hats. Of the razzamatazz of the modern podium presentation, however, there is not a trace.

In those early days, when cycling was still establishing itself on the wider sporting stage, it was a strictly all-male affair; a woman's role was to cheer on the riders or wait dutifully at home for them to return. As the race grew in popularity, though, it became clear that some more formalised presentation was necessary, and women were selected to present these if they fulfilled two simple criteria: that they were under the age of 30 and smaller than the (often diminutive) riders. Sexual politics played its part too – the presence of women added a veneer of glamour to the sport, while simultaneously presenting females as purely adjuncts to successful and virile men.

The rise of the podium, with its protocols and presentations, became more formalised in the post-World War II era. As with most traditions relating to cycling's Grand Tours, the Tour de France paved the way, taking full advantage of the fortuitous coincidence that the year the race returned, 1947, was also the year that Miss France was crowned for the first time. With beauty pageants on the up, organisers of the Tour invited local beauty queens to meet the riders, a newspaper-worthy occasion that must have benefitted both events.

The women's function was, however, strictly to be decorative: there was to be no suggestion that women might be as competitive as men on their machines. Indeed, competitive women's cycling had been banned in France after 1912 and was not recognised again until 1950. It seems plausible that by presenting women as being anything but 'Giants of the Road', the Tour was making a point about where exactly they belonged.

The modern Tour hostess – a hotly contested job that sees thousands of yearly applicants being whittled down to the handful who actually appear in the podium – has to ferry VIPs from place to place, handle public relations, ensure the podium protocol runs smoothly, and be a silent beauty. Fraternising with riders is strictly forbidden, though it does happen and many successful partnerships have resulted – for instance, American George Hincapie married Melanie Simonneau in 2003, though she lost her job as a result of their relationship. There have been numerous unfortunate incidents too – riders groping hostesses, hostesses refusing to kiss the yellow-jersey winner – but things usually go according to plan.

Podium and race rules dictate that the jerseys that are presented daily to the leaders of the various competitions are not standard – instead they zip up the back for ease and speed of presentation. These prizes are presented in strict order: first the stage winner, then the jerseys – the overall race leader, the points competition, King of the Mountains and finally, best young rider. The podium itself is a truck that follows the race and is erected, along with the metal barriers, finishing stands, gantries and other structures, by the army of staff who help to ensure the logistical nightmare that is a major cycling race runs without incident.

For all its convoluted razzamatazz, however, the flowers and the local dignitaries remain, linking the sport back to its earliest, less formal presentations.

French cyclist Jean Robic, shown with Miss France, after winning the final stage of the 1947 Tour de France.

Cuddly lion

It's one of the most coveted prizes in all of cycling. Bright yellow and irresistibly cute, the cuddly toy lion has been handed out to the holder of the yellow jersey at the end of every Tour de France stage since 1987.

Although it may seem an odd trophy for hardened cyclists, the lion is by no means the strangest prize in cycling – that honour is held by the live piglet presented to the winner of the French race Tro-Bro Léon. Other races offer other slightly leftfield rewards, too, such as the now-defunct Haribo Classic, the winner of which would receive his weight in sweets; the sprint race, Kuurne–Brussels–Kuurne, which offers the chance to win a stuffed donkey; and in Italy, the Tirreno–Adriatico ('Race Between Two Seas'), whose victor gets to brandish a large gilded trident, in honour of the Roman god of the sea, Neptune.

The real attraction of such prizes for the event organisers is, however, the sponsorship and press coverage associated with them. For instance, the Tour de France lion is sponsored by one of France's major banks, Crédit Lyonnais (LCL), and they pay handsomely for the privilege of handing out the yellow lions on the winner's podium – to the tune of US$15 million to become the sole yellow-jersey sponsor in 1987, a figure that was triple the size of the sum paid for their original three-year contract in 1981. That figure rose to US$20 million in the 1990s. The benefits of sponsorship cut both ways and it's easy to understand why global corporations such as Coca-Cola want to sponsor the third-biggest live sporting event in the world: its huge roadside audiences, massive global television audience and three-week duration all help the Tour to deliver a big bang for a sponsor's buck.

Cycling's business model is an unusual one in major sport. With the event free to view live, there are no lucrative ticket receipts, although companies sell packages that enable spectators to sit in the stands to watch the final kilometre of major races. Nor are proceeds from the lucrative rights to television coverage shared with competing teams, as they are for football and American sports, so cycling relies heavily on sponsorship – which is why riders' jerseys resemble multi-coloured billboards.

Since the sport first became competitive, teams and individuals have been sponsored by companies involved in the manufacture of bicycles and their components. However, by the 1950s and the rise of automotive transport, investment was waning, and with it cyclists' wages. The top riders were thus forced to look for *extrasportif* support. The appeal for those companies that bought in to riders and the sport was that the jersey, not the bicycle, was the main focus of their advertising. The first rider to wear a jersey advertising a product not directly related to cycling was the Italian, Fiorenzo Magni, who in 1954 turned to Nivea.

The rugged-faced Magni seemed an unlikely fit with a women's face-cream manufacturer, but the cyclist had contacts with the men behind the brand and he understood the commercial value they both might gain from a mutually lucrative sponsorship deal. However, despite getting Nivea on board to sponsor the Magni team, the Italian national champion was soon in trouble – the organisers of the 1954 Paris–Roubaix refused to let Magni into the race unless he wore his national champion's jersey. In response, countryman Fausto Coppi, sensing how important the Nivea deal was for the future of cycling, refused to race unless Magni wore his Nivea jersey. Thus the battle was won, and the complexion of cycling sponsorship was changed forever.

Irish cyclist Stephen Roche holding the
cuddly lion as race leader at the 1987
Tour de France, the first time it made an
appearance at the Tour, and the same
year he won cycling's Triple Crown.

If the Tour de France remains the ultimate three-week stage race, the Tour of Flanders and Paris–Roubaix are its one-day equivalents. Known as the 'cobbled classics', these are the toughest races in the cycling calendar.

The oldest of the cobbled one-day races is Paris–Roubaix, which dates back to 1896. Often featuring in the Tours of the 1900s, the route may be flat as a pancake but it is nevertheless leg-sappingly difficult thanks to the granite setts over which large sections of the race are run.

The Roubaix came about thanks to the construction of a velodrome there in 1895. Wondering how best to promote it, two of its backers, Théodore Vienne and Maurice Perez (both textile manufacturers and racers in the area), hit upon the idea of a bicycle race that started in the capital (as it did until 1967, when the start line moved 87km north to Compiègne) and finished at the velodrome.

In order to assess the route they enlisted the help of Victor Breyer, editor of *Le Vélo*. This he did, both at the race's inception and in the aftermath of World War I, when the landscape had been brutalised by the ravages of war: 'Shell-holes one after the other, with no gaps, outlines of trenches, barbed wire cut into one thousand pieces; unexploded shells on the roadside, here and there, graves. Crosses bearing a jaunty tricolour are the only light relief.' A gruesome scene indeed, and one that caused his companion on that ride – cyclist Eugène Christophe – to declare: 'This really is the hell of the north.'

Such is the difficulty of the race that even after the carnage of war had been cleared the name stuck, and Paris–Roubaix became known as the 'Hell of the North'. *Sunday in Hell* was the title of a 1976 documentary on the race. The main cause of difficulty along the route is the number of cobbled roads. These are not the well-laid, elegant cobbled boulevards of Paris or the well-used cobbles of Flanders, but heavy-set, rough working roads that date back to the days of Napoleon. In the dry, a string of treacherous potholes lie in wait to puncture even the best-prepared tyres and send up clouds of dust that choke the riders' lungs and eyes. In the wet, they are even more dangerous, their slippery surface bringing down even the most adept of bike handlers.

In response to complaints over the years, *Les Amis de Paris–Roubaix*, a volunteer organisation, has worked tirelessly since 1983 to maintain the cobbles – each one a 15cm (6in) granite cube bedded on sand – but the race is still a tough one and riders who have experienced it say that each cobble is like a hammer blow, sending shockwaves through every joint in the body.

Despite this, riders return again and again to try to win the famous cobblestone trophy given to the winner. As Dutch rider Theo de Rooij said after abandoning the 1985 race: 'It's a shitty race! We ride like animals, we don't even have the time to take a piss so we piss in our shorts – it's a pile of shit.' But would he come back and ride again? 'Of course, it's the most beautiful race in the world.'

The odd compulsion that makes uncomfortable races popular is not restricted to Paris-Roubaix: the most important race in Flanders, the Ronde van Vlaanderen (or La Ronde) – started in 1913 and contested every year since 1919, making it the race with the longest uninterrupted run – adds short, sharp climbs known as *hellingen* to its cobbled roads. However, here the cobbles are smoother and more rounded through regular use than the rougher ones of northern France, giving them the nickname *kinderkoppen* or baby's heads – though riders still experience a somewhat bumpy ride.

Mr. Paris–Roubaix, Roger de
Vlaeminck, races over the rain-
soaked cobbles in the 1973 race.

77 Hairpin bends

Cycling has Alphonse Steinès, a journalist at *L'Auto* at the start of the 20th century, to thank for the introduction of high mountain peaks into cycle racing. He envisaged a stage of the Tour de France that would incorporate the 'Circle of Death', several of the highest and most inaccessible mountains in the French Pyrenees. His boss, Henri Desgrange, thought the idea ridiculous – then most of the routes through the mountains were little more than cart tracks – but rather than dismiss it out of hand, he sent Steinès to discover whether the plan was indeed feasible.

Although the Frenchman's ascent of the Tourmalet was torrid – he was caught in a blizzard and, forced to abandon his vehicle, crossed the summit on foot – Steinès was convinced that a Pyrenean stage was possible and, upon reaching safety, thus sent a brief telegram to the offices of *L'Auto*: 'Crossed the Tourmalet. Stop. Very good road. Stop. Perfectly feasible. Stop. Signed Steinès.' And so the 1910 Tour saw itself racing over the Tourmalet.

The first man over the summit was Octave Lapize, though he was not terribly impressed by this new test of cycling endeavour, telling journalists before he had even dismounted from his bicycle: 'You can tell Desgrange: no one can ask men to make an effort like this. I've had enough.' Then, with a cry of 'assassins!' he assumed his slow, torturous progress to the finish. The Tourmalet was retained, despite these protests, and featured in possibly the hardest-ever stage in cycling history when, during the 1926 race, the peloton covered 323km (200 miles) over seven mountain passes. Ridden in appalling weather conditions, the riders accomplished the climbs with icicles hanging from their moustaches and handlebars.

The Alps followed a year later, in 1927, with an assault on the Col du Galibier. When the race finished at the summit of the climb in 2011, it was the highest finish the race had ever seen. Though not the loftiest pass in the Alps, for many it is the greatest climb in the Tour de France, and since 1947 the first rider over the top has been awarded the *Souvenir Henri Desgrange* – named after the newspaper owner who wrote of his favourite climb: 'Are these men not winged, who today climbed to heights where even eagles don't go?' A similar prize is awarded for the highest climb of the Giro d'Italia, where it is called the *Cima Coppi* (*cima* meaning 'summit' or 'peak') after the legendary Fausto Coppi.

Among the most iconic climbs in the Tour are Alpe d'Huez and Mont Ventoux. The former is famed for its 21 hairpin bends that loop up the mountain to the summit finish, each furnished with posts declaring the names of most, if not all, the winners, whereas Mont Ventoux is known as an anomaly, standing distinct from any mountain range, its exposed slopes and often oppressive heat making it one of the fiercest challenges in cycling.

The real climber's race, however, is considered to be the Giro d'Italia. With major ascents in the Apennines, Dolomites and Alps to choose from, course designers have been able to send the race over some of the toughest terrain in Europe. The Giro's first mountain stage finished at the Alpine village of Sestrière in 1911, and since then, the race has included such iconic summits as the Monte Zoncolan and the Stelvio Pass – the *Cima Coppi* par excellence, the title given to the highest point ever reached in the race, standing at over 2743m (9000ft). However, the epic ascent of the Gavia in 1988 – when, battered by a blizzard, American Andy Hampsten sealed the first-ever victory in the race by a non-European and, according to the *Gazzetta dello Sport*, 'the big men cried' – is probably the most famous in modern cycling history.

An aerial view of the mountain roads that climb the Alpe d'Huez from the 1992 Tour de France. The hairpin bends of the great climbs like the Alpe d'Huez, the Gavia and the Stelvio Pass create spectacular bike racing.

Carpet tacks

From the earliest days of competitive cycling, the risk of pneumaticide has threatened every rider's dreams of glory.

In the 1905 Tour de France, *L'Auto* reported that 125kg (276lb) of nails were scattered on the roads between Besançon and Nancy. This caused chaos – one of the leading riders picked up no fewer than 15 punctures and, at a time when all repairs had to be made by the cyclists themselves, it was devastating. Although Henri Desgrange suspected that the Michelin brothers were behind the attack, in order to demonstrate the superiority of their tyres, the real culprits were in fact fans protesting the exclusion from the race of a local favourite.

Thereafter, sabotage became commonplace, and not just during the Tour de France; the 1914 Giro d'Italia started in chaos when thousands of tacks were strewn across the roads of the opening stage by angry locals annoyed by the presence of a bike race on their doorstep. This caused the entire race to grind to a halt and it seemed the Giro was over before it had even begun.

Nails or tacks as a weapon of choice for protestors have the advantage of being cheap, easily available and utterly deadly, but there have been other types of protests over the years. These are sometimes aimed at or caused by individual racers, but often the actions simply make use of one of the biggest sporting events in the world to get a point across.

Examples of a more personal nature include the attack on Eddy Merckx during the 1975 Tour de France that saw an angry spectator stepping out into the road and punching the great Belgian rider. Merckx crossed the finish line vomiting with pain and would never wear the yellow jersey again. Lance Armstrong was regularly spat at and called a '*dopeur*' by race fans who doubted the

American was all he seemed, and Team Sky riders have also endured name-calling and been showered with beer and other, more noxious, liquids. In 2000, a nightclub owner protesting the loss of his licence tried to impede one rider's progress by throwing hay bales at him.

Sometimes riders retaliate, and one of the most famous images in cycling is that of Frenchman Bernard Hinault throwing a punch at the 1984 Paris–Nice race. During the event, shipyard workers protesting pay and conditions had blocked the route, and Hinault had ploughed straight into them. Nowadays, fortunately, protestors hoping to use a cycling race to raise the profile of a campaign will usually come to an arrangement with the organisers and simply wave their banners by the side of the road.

Riders themselves are not above going on strike as a response to perceived injustices or to protest against unsafe race conditions. Most famously, the riders of the 1998 Tour de France staged a sit-in protest in the middle of stage 12 after a series of night-time police raids. Although they subsequently rode to the finish line, the race was a bad-tempered affair, marred by the Festina doping scandal.

Despite the availability of more advanced methods of race sabotage, however, the humble tack is still in use. In 2012, hundreds of them were scattered over a 1km (1094-yard) stretch of the descent of the Mur de Péguère, an incident that earned Sir Bradley Wiggins, wearing the yellow jersey, the nickname 'the Gentleman' when he asked the peloton to stop riding and allow riders who had punctured to catch up. Worryingly, the trend for using tacks is also now spreading to the amateur side of the sport, and there have been widely reported incidents of sabotage during amateur sportive rides in Scotland and Wales.

From the very earliest days of cycling racing, pneumaticide from carpet tacks has ended many riders' races prematurely. Levi Leipheimer points to where carpet tacks had been thrown across the road, causing him and Robert Kišerlovski to crash during the 2012 Tour de France.

79 Team car

There have always been support vehicles in professional cycling, but their function over the years has altered radically. Strict rules about the use of team cars were in force during the very first Tour, when any vehicle found to be following a rider with spare bicycles or food would be disqualified. By the 1930s, the rules on allowing a rider to seek assistance for repairs had been relaxed and team cars were permitted to carry spare components, though using a car for drafting could still see a rider excluded from the race. By the 1940s, team cars were a firm fixture in most major races.

In the modern Tour there are some 250 cars in the convoy, including: yellow Mavic neutral service vehicles (*see* pp. 176–177); the race director's bright-red car, plus those of the assistant director and race steward, all of which travel at the front of the race, ahead of the peloton; a fleet of press and sponsors' cars and motorbikes – some with photographers, some supplying water, one supplying time checks; police vehicles and the *Garde Républicaine*; and the team cars. Together, this impressive cavalcade greatly outnumbers the 198 contestants.

Other notable personages and their automobiles include the president of the race jury, who travels behind the peloton to check for rule violations; the race doctor, who travels in a convertible so he can lean out of the car and treat injured riders more easily; and, bringing up the rear, are the infamous broom wagon (*see* pp. 180–181) and the official *fin de course* (end-of-the-race) vehicle.

For the riders themselves, the most important of these vehicles are the team support cars, which travel in a set order in the motorcade for each day's stage. This is determined by their team leader's overall position in the race – if your rider is leading, you take position one, and so on. So, achieving a high position on the general classification is as important for team cars as it is for riders; the closer you are to the action, the more easily you can assist a rider who crashes or gets a puncture.

For the Tour, two team cars support their riders. One – driven by the *directeur sportif*, who makes the decisions about race tactics – usually stays with the team leader while the second car rides with other team members. There is a mechanic in each car, and passengers ready to provide sustenance and information alongside on-the-fly medical assistance, a new bike or spare wheel and general encouragement.

The newcomer in the support-vehicle paddock is the team bus. Fitted with massage tables, comfortable seating, washing machines and kitchens, these mobile palaces provide some much-welcome luxury in the tough world of bike racing. The trend for ever-more lavishly appointed vehicles was started by the Team Sky bus – nicknamed the 'Death Star' thanks to its black livery – and these enable riders to start their recovery the second they step aboard.

Some of the vehicles, however, cause problems. After a spate of accidents in recent years, including a particularly nasty crash involving a press car, Johnny Hoogerland and a barbed-wire fence in the 2011 Tour de France, there are now strict rules governing vehicles that accompany the race. All drivers are required to undergo training and to give a clear picture of their movements in the race – for example, the driver of a press car must tell organisers whether they have any plans to overtake the peloton.

Despite the odd regrettable incident, however, the cars, buses and press bikes do, in general, enhance the experience for riders and viewers alike, and are now an important part of the Tour de France and most other major bike races.

The team vehicles of the 1951
Tour de France – all part of
the spectacle of the race.

80 Mavic car

Among the team cars and other support vehicles that follow the riders during a race, there is one that has no loyalty to any team: the Mavic or neutral support car, which is there to help riders who suffer a mechanical mishap – most usually a flat tyre – during the race.

Standing for *Manufacture d'Articles Vélocipédiques Idoux et Chanel* (loosely translated as 'manufacture of items for vélocipèdes, by Idoux and Chanel') and named after its two founders, Mavic began by manufacturing mudguards and aluminium wheel rims, the latter of which were tested in secret by Antonin Magne at the 1934 Tour de France, when they were painted to resemble the wooden rims that were the only type allowed in the race. Magne subsequently took the yellow jersey with a lead of more than 20 minutes, and sales of the rims soared.

Although the Tour de France had changed its draconian rules about rider assistance in the 1930s, the idea for neutral support wasn't conceived until 40 years later and only came about after an incident at the 1972 Critérium du Dauphiné, when a Mavic driver offered his own car to a team manager who had broken down. The following year, a neutral and free repair car was trialled at the 1973 Paris–Nice, riding at the head of the race and relaying information to all other support vehicles by radio. This was an immediate success and saved the day for numerous riders who would otherwise lose a race or be forced to abandon it because of mechanical problems. Moreover, Mavic mechanics took their responsibilities seriously, undergoing training to make their wheel changes as fast and flawless as possible – by the 1980s they could change a back wheel in an average 15 seconds and a front wheel in 10 seconds.

Since their advent, Mavic cars have pulled countless cyclists out of ditches and made thousands of quick wheel changes, especially at the most puncture-prone event of them all, Paris–Roubaix, although on the pavé sectors support is generally provided by volunteers or staff in the crowd holding spare wheels, and by neutral service motorbikes rather than cars. Other tales of incidents in which Mavic cars have saved the day are more unusual. In 2010, for instance, German rider Jens Voigt, having crashed hard on the descent of the Col de Peyresourde with no support in sight, was saved by a child's bike supplied by a neutral car that had followed a youth event earlier in the day. Having grabbed the bike – complete with toe straps – the strapping German pedalled for 20km (12.4 miles) until he could swap it for an adult-sized ride, and went on to finish the stage and stay in the Tour.

The familiar yellow cars have also provided support for mountain-biking races since the 1980s and currently attend more than 200 events, both amateur and professional, around the world. As French rider Laurent Jalabert recalls: 'You got to know the people in the cars, it wasn't just a case of the car being behind you [Jalabert would use the presence of the Mavic car between himself and the peloton to gauge how much time he had in a breakaway]. You could always ask the car for a bottle of water on a hot stage of the Tour.'

The Mavic neutral service car, providing support for all riders, has been a part of cycling since the 1973 Paris–Nice. Here a car makes its way through the dust at the 2011 Paris–Roubaix.

81 Chalkboard

During the rest of the year, she's a financial risk analyst, but every summer Frenchwoman Claire Pedrono climbs on the back of a motorbike and weaves through the speeding peloton. Claire is the official *Ardoisière* at the Tour de France.

In 2010, when the former multiple cycling champion of Brittany climbed aboard the *moto* for the first time, she also became the first woman to hold the all-important chalkboard in the Tour. Until that day, the *Ardoisière* had always been an *Ardoisièr*.

The role of the blackboard has traditionally been one of the most important in the race. It is on this black square (*ardoise* is the French word for 'slate') that information about time gaps between groups of riders and the race numbers of those in a breakaway will be chalked. There are even official UCI-sanctioned dimensions for the blackboard – 40 x 55cm (16 x 22in) – and, just to underline how important the task is, the blackboard man or woman is considered to be a race official.

But surely modern bike racing should be relying on GPS technology to calculate accurate time gaps? Well, it does, in the form of iOS and Android apps, such as the official Tour Tracker, which uses bike-mounted GPS transponders (not to be confused with the timing chips each rider also carries to accurately record their finishing time) to track the riders in real time and send the information to any *directeur sportif* with a smartphone. However, on the road, in time-honoured tradition, timings are taken with a stopwatch and a timing motorbike. It's almost laughably low-tech – the motorbike simply rides

up to the front group of riders, stops and sets the stopwatch ticking until the peloton arrives. Time gaps are relayed to the race commissaires, who then relay the time gaps via race radio, at which point the *Ardoisière* or *Ardoisièr* writes the information on the chalkboard and relays it to the peloton.

The *Ardoisière* or *Ardoisièr* is a pillion passenger and is completely dependent on their pilot to navigate them through the race as they need to be able to twist around to display the chalkboard to the cyclists behind them. To ride a motorbike the length of the Tour takes skill and precision, be it riding slowly and with complete control as the riders toil up a mountain climb or flying down the descents at speeds of up to 150kph (93mph). For this reason, *moto* riders – whether they are course officials or carrying press photographers or other personnel – must take an initial training course at the motorcycle police training centre near Paris, followed by a refresher course every two years. They are the only civilians allowed to access this elite school, which trains them to the very high standards required to do the job; penalties for poor driving are harsh, with riders facing lifetime exclusion from the race.

However, it seems the days of the blackboard and chalk are numbered. In 2013, a number of races experimented with using a motorbike-mounted electronic display to flash up race information. The Tour de France, however, is keeping faith with the chalkboard and the history and tradition it represents, for now at least, enabling Claire to continue on her yellow-clad way, the only woman who actually takes part in the race.

Claire Pedrono, the first *Ardoisière*, records the time gaps between the breakaway and the peloton on her trusty slate during the 2010 Tour de France.

82 Broom wagon

Exactly as its name suggests, the purpose of the broom wagon is to 'sweep up' riders too injured, exhausted, sick or demoralised to go on. No rider wants to take a ride in it, an experience one French professional described as being the most humiliating and humbling of his career.

Henri Desgrange introduced the original *voiture balai* – a van with a broom poked through the back door handles – in the 1910 Tour de France, the year that the French race ventured into the Pyrenees for the first time – and they have been a race feature ever since. Of the various vehicles that have been used as a broom wagon, the Citroen H van, nicknamed Le Tube, was the most iconic iteration. With its squared nose and ridged sides, it's immediately recognisable from race photos of the late 1940s. After Citroen ceased production in 1982, Le Tube was replaced by a standard recreational vehicle – though the common dread of having to go over the finish line in it remains the same.

Once a rider has made the unenviable decision to abandon the race and climb into the *voiture balai* he is stripped of his race numbers by race commissaires. There is more than an element of public humiliation in the gesture, as is described by Graham Jones, who was 20th

in the 1981 Tour de France, when he wrote: 'I defy any rider to say that he hasn't shed a tear at climbing into the Tour broom wagon. Maybe not immediately but at some time in that journey to the finish.'

Indeed, such is the dread of riding in the broom wagon that sometimes just the sight of it alone is enough to galvanise a rider to extraordinary feats. Fans of cycling will know the name Paul Sherwen from his commentary work, but less well known is the fact that Sherwen was also a professional rider who, in his last Tour de France in 1986, rode over six mountain passes alone after a terrible crash nearly put him out of the race. Cycling with the broom wagon at his heels for all that time, Sherwen finished the stage outside the time limit, which meant automatic disqualification from the race. Lenient officials, however, were so impressed by his courage that they overturned the rule and allowed him to finish his final Tour.

Nowadays, a rider who abandons the race is more likely to climb into his team car, often in tears – think of Chris Froome on a rain-sodden day in the 2014 Tour de France when he was forced to climb off his bike after breaking his wrist – yet the broom wagon lives on, another anachronism linking cycling's past and present.

The *camion balai*, or broom wagon, sweeps up riders who had abandoned the race during the 1960 Tour de France.

83 *Flamme rouge*

Every race, for whatever sport, needs a start and a finish line. A simple chalk stroke or a painted line will suffice at the start – and still does in every race, from a local criterium to the Tour de France – but what about the end of the race?

In the same way that track athletes are notified that they are starting their final lap by the ringing of a bell, cycling gives riders a visual indication that they are entering the last kilometre of their effort by displaying a triangle of red cloth, commonly known as the *flamme rouge*. Meaning 'red flame' and also known as the 'red kite', the *flamme rouge* is usually suspended over the road and was first introduced in 1906 (a year that is famous for a number of other firsts in the Tour, being the first time the race crossed the boundaries of France and the first time that stages didn't depart from the same place as the one where they had finished).

Quite how the *flamme rouge* came about is unclear, but it seems possible that it was introduced as an attempt to engineer a hard-fought finish between riders who now had some indication that they were close to the finish and would push extra hard to achieve victory. Whether or not this is the case, what is certain is that a new breed of cyclist subsequently began to appear: the *finisseur*.

A *finisseur* (in English a 'finisher') is the type of rider who has the strength, speed and guile to attack the peloton alone over the closing stages of a race. The last kilometre, demarcated by the *flamme rouge*, is the *finisseur's* favourite territory and is the stretch of road that has produced some of the most notable characters. These included during the 1960s and '70s the Belgian Walter Godefroot – who would go on to have a distinguished career in team management with Telekom (later T-Mobile) – nicknamed *Le Finisseur* for his abilities to steal stages from under the noses of the peloton, which enabled him to become the first winner on the Champs-Élysées in 1975, winning the last stage in his final Tour.

In addition to being a distance marker, the *flamme rouge* can also signal the adrenaline rush of a pure sprint, when the teams of the fastest men in the race jockey for position to lead out their sprinters in the headlong rush for glory. For that reason it can also be one of the most dangerous spots in any race as huge and terrifying crashes inside those final 1000m (1093 yards) are not uncommon. The *flamme rouge* itself, which these days is a sponsored inflatable arch or banner, can also pose a danger, as Adam Yates discovered in the 2016 Tour when the inflatable banner became unplugged accidently, breaking free and wrapping itself around a Mavic bike and several riders. Yates came off his bike and ended the stage in 73rd place, thanks to the delay.

Despite the problems, however, the *flamme rouge* is very much a part of the tradition and culture of the Tour, and seems set to stay.

The welcome sight of the *flamme rouge* tells the riders they're just one kilometre from the finish line. This was a less welcome sight for Adam Yates, however, during the 2016 Tour after the inflatable *flamme rouge* collapsed on to him.

The Champs-Elysées

The Champs-Elysées is as familiar to the most casual cycling fan as it is to the millions of tourists who flock to Paris each year. At 70m (230ft) wide and nearly 2km (1.2 miles) long, it connects the Place de la Concorde at one end with the Place Charles de Gaulle at the other.

Conceived as the most beautiful boulevard in the world, it is renowned as the iconic finish of the biggest cycling event in the world, the Tour de France. Yet the race has only finished there since 1975, when French President Valéry Giscard d'Estaing finally granted race organisers permission to close the boulevard for one Sunday every July. Before that, from its inception in 1903 until 1967, the race had finished initially with a circuit of the velodrome at Parc des Princes, before this was moved to the velodrome in the Parc de Vincennes. Thus many of the greatest winners of the race, such as Eddy Merckx, Fausto Coppi and Jacques Anquetil, have never ridden the cobbles of the Champs-Élysées.

The now-traditional finish takes the form of a circuit race and has become an unofficial sprinter's world championships, with the fastest men in the sport vying to add a victory there to their *palmarès* (list of race wins). This results in an incredibly competitive environment that sometimes ends in spills as well as thrills, as was the case in 1991 when the 'Tashkent Terror' Djamolidine Abdoujaparov was involved in a horrifying crash as he sprinted for the line wearing the green jersey as leader on the points competition. Despite the accident, however, more than 20 minutes later, with the help of his team, Abdoujaparov finally made it to the podium to claim the first of his three green jerseys.

Since 2013, the traditional loop of the Champs-Elysées has incorporated the Arc de Triomphe, the great triumphal arch that already had its own place in cycling history: it was here that Britain's James Moore lined up with 119 other riders to contest the first-ever road race, Paris–Rouen, in 1869, an event Moore won in 10 hours 40 minutes. Only 34 riders finished that year, one of whom was 'Miss America', an unknown Briton who was the only female in the race and remained the only woman to ride in competition on the Champs-Elysées until the 1980s, when the Grande Boucle Féminine Internationale finished on the same circuit as the men's race.

Since 2014, the Champs-Elysées has also hosted one of the most prestigious one-day women's races in the world: La Course, which attracts the best women cyclists in the professional peloton to one of the most iconic avenues in the world.

Though the tradition of finishing the Tour along the Champs-Elysées is relatively recent, the venue has quickly become one of the most beautiful and well-known sporting arenas in the world. In the words of the current race director Christian Prudhomme: 'The union between the Champs-Elysées and Le Tour is a partnership that everybody knows about. Nobody can imagine a finish of Le Tour anywhere else than on the Champs-Elysées.'

The women's peloton passes the Arc de Triomphe during the first edition of La Course in 2014.

85 Massage table

Every great champion has had his favourite soigneur – fulfilling the roles of masseur, nutritionist, advisor and therapist.

The word 'soigneur' derives from the French verb *soigner* – to take care of – and it is up to them to provide, among other things: clean cycling kit, filled musettes and bidons and a reviving massage at the end of a hard day's racing. Their role doesn't stop there, however, and some soigneurs have also guided their riders to glory – as was the case for Guillaume Michiels, who worked with Eddy Merckx. Some have broken boundaries, as Emma O'Reilly did when she gave evidence against Lance Armstrong; and occasionally they have broken the law, such as when Festina's Willy Voet carried drugs in his car. He was subsequently busted.

Soigneurs have been part of the racing scene since the earliest days of professional cycling, sporting the yellow clothing introduced by the French Alcyon cycling team in order to make them more visible, that appeared several years before the yellow jersey was first awarded in 1919. Originally, soigneurs worked for several riders rather than focusing on just one and it wasn't until the 1940s that cyclists such as Fausto Coppi started employing their own personal ones. This led to some famous pairings, including those of the French rider Louison Bobet and Raymond le Bert in the 1950s. Bobet's soigneur was a former professional road racer, and he revolutionised Bobet's approach to diet and training.

By contrast, other soigneurs have been more akin to witch doctors, dispensing bizarre and arcane nutritional advice to their charges. In the 1960s, Tom Simpson's soigneur Gus Naessens was typical of this approach, cooking up cattle feed into a kind of porridge for his rider's bidons, based on the theory that it would sit in a cyclist's stomach and thus prevent his body from utilising energy that would be better used by his legs.

Fortunately, this kind of pseudo-scientific approach to diet has now disappeared from the sport and a modern soigneur is most likely to come from a background in sports science or massage therapy. Moreover, in an effort to professionalise their standing in the sport, the UCI introduced a soigneur-training course in 2013 to supply support personnel with the skills required for the increasingly complex and scientific demands of the sport.

Chief among these is massage therapy. Cyclists have always relied on massage after hour upon hour of churning the pedals, and its benefits are numerous: it increases blood flow, flushes out toxins, reduces soreness and can also break down the adhesions that occur when stressed muscles experience micro-tears, thus restoring the full range of motion. In addition, a few minutes on the massage table provide a private moment for a rider, away from the stresses of a race and the media circus that surrounds it.

The massage table hasn't always been the site of such wholesome activity, however, featuring instead in some rather shady tales. Among these is the story from 1905 of Louis Trousselier, who, having pocketed 25,000 francs in prize money and lucrative post-race contracts for winning the Tour de France, entered a cabin at the Buffalo velodrome and spent the whole night playing dice on a massage table. He clearly played dice rather less well than he cycled, since he left the massage room without a sou in his pocket and, though he vowed he'd come back and win it all again the following year, he never did. He also never rode as well at the Tour again. Riders beware!

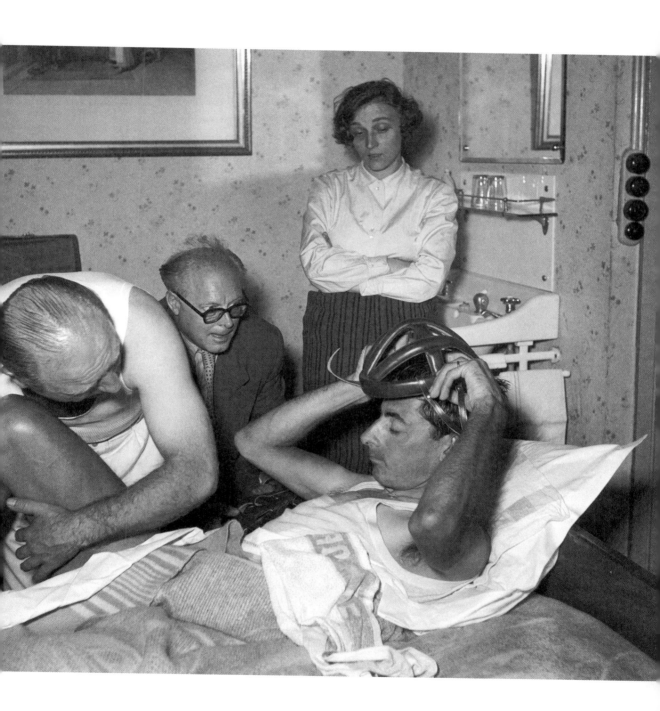

Fausto Coppi receives a massage
during the 1951 Tour de France.

86 UCI

From bad-tempered beginnings, the *Union Cycliste Internationale* (UCI) has risen to become the world governing body of cycling.

In 1892, Henry Sturmey (of Sturmey-Archer 3-speed-hub fame) set up the International Cycling Association (ICA) with the intention of organising the World Championships. Accordingly, Sturmey met representatives from France, Germany, Holland, Italy and Canada and the first worlds were held a year later in Chicago, USA.

Sturmey was keen to enshrine the principle of amateurism in the organisation but the ICA proved ineffective as a governing body. Bans on professional riders were not observed by other nations, and the influential *Union Vélocipèdique Française* (UVF) was excluded after a dispute over amateurism.

Unhappy about the role played by the autocratic Sturmey and the domination of the ICA by the Anglo-Saxon voting block – all nations were allowed one vote except Britain, which had one each for England, Scotland and Wales – the UVF seized their chance when the World Championships were announced for Paris in 1900. After an acrimonious meeting of the ICA in the French capital in 1990, the French, Belgian, Italian, Swiss and American associations, in a move orchestrated by the UVF, announced both their withdrawal from the ICA and the formation of a new body, the UCI. It was this latter group that went on to organise the World Championships later that year. To add insult to injury, Britain was excluded from the UCI until 1903 for failure to attend their inaugural meeting. After 1903 they were allowed to join, but were only permitted to vote as one nation, rather than four as they had previously.

By the 1950s, the UCI was responsible for organising the cyclocross and indoor cycling World Championships, with mountain biking and BMX gaining representation in the 1990s. In 1965 the International Olympic Committee (IOC) required the organisation to split into two separate entities to represent amateur and professional cycling, a distinction that disappeared in 1992 when amateur status for Olympians was dropped.

Today, the UCI represents 174 cycling nations grouped under five continental federations from their head-quarters in Switzerland. There have been to date 10 presidents of the organisation, and in 2013, Australian cyclist Tracey Gaudry made history when she was appointed its first female vice-president. Not restricted to road racing, the UCI is the governing body for all cycling disciplines, promoting and developing the sport at all levels and ensuring sportsmanship and fair play.

However, despite their laudable tenets, the UCI itself is no stranger to making controversial decisions or becoming embroiled in scandal. Attempts to ban two-way radio communication have angered teams, and arbitrary rule changes and outright banning of equipment and riding positions have left some scratching their heads. More seriously, there have been allegations of bribery over the inclusion of keirin in the Olympic Games and suspicions and speculation regarding doping cover-ups, particularly with regard to the Lance Armstrong affair.

Despite this, however, there is no doubt that the organisation does have an important part to play in the sport of cycling, whether for better or for worse.

The *Union Cycliste Internationale* has been the world governing body for cycling since 1900. UCI Vice President Tracey Gaudry and President Brian Cookson are shown standing on the start line prior to the Women's Road Race at the 2016 Rio Olympic Games.

Track Cycling

87 Velodrome

The biggest sport in America in the 1880s wasn't baseball (the 'national pastime'), it was cycling, with huge crowds flocking to Madison Square Garden to watch the six-day racing. Indeed, such was the popularity and lucrative nature of the event that by the 1920s the cyclists who took part were the best-paid sportsmen in the country.

The French for 'bicycle race tracks', *velodromes* were first built in the mid–late 19th century. Consisting of banked oval wooden tracks – two straights joined by curved ends – these were used for cycling as well as some other sports and were located both indoors and outdoors.

The explosion in popularity of cycling at the end of the 19th century led to the sport of track cycling, and tracks soon sprang up across America and Europe. Sometimes with a concrete, asphalt or even dirt or grass surface, these varied in length from 333.3m to 500m, or even more. Some are smaller, too, such as the Kuipke velodrome in Belgium, which has hosted the famous Six Days of Ghent event since 1922 and is a mere 166m (182 yards), giving it a uniquely intimate atmosphere. Competition tracks have now been standardised at 250m.

The title of the oldest surviving velodrome in the world goes to Preston Park in Brighton, England, which was dug out by hand by members of the British Army in 1877. Laid with a cinder track, it was hazardous to any rider who suffered a crash there – the cinders would have to be removed from an injured rider's lacerations with hot water and a scrubbing brush – and eventually the surface was replaced with tarmac in 1936.

France boasts the greatest number of velodromes in the world and among them several of the most famous. These include a favoured haunt of the American writer Ernest Hemingway, the Vélodrome d'Hiver (or Vel d'Hiv, as it's known) in Paris, which opened its doors in 1902 and hosted six-day races alongside other events such as roller-skating marathons. It has a darker reputation, too, having played a role in the round-up and deportation of Jews from France in World War II. The Buffalo velodrome, also in Paris and named after the American showman Buffalo Bill Cody, who often appeared there with his Wild West show featuring sharpshooter Annie Oakley, is best known for being the venue for the first official hour record in 1893. A hundred years later, the Bordeaux velodrome – the baby of the bunch that opened its doors in 1989 – was the site where in one extraordinary 16-month period in 1993–1994 the world hour record fell five times.

However, the most famous venue for the hour record is Velodromo Vigorelli in Milan, the wooden boards of which were once known as the *pista magica* or the magic track. Opened in 1935, its Modernist structure also housed a bicycle shop and it was here that Fausto Coppi set his hour record during World War II, shortly after the track had been rocked by aerial bombardment. The track has lain fallow since 1999 but, inspired by restoration work undertaken at the historic Herne Hill velodrome in London (a Victorian facility built in the early 1890s), it will soon open its *piste* once more to cyclists.

Many of the most famous velodrome tracks – including the Vigorelli and hour record-breaking tracks in Mexico and Norway – were designed by German architects Schuermann, who have been in the business since the 1920s. Moreover, it was Schuermann who popularised the use of the African hardwood Afzelia (colloquially known as 'doussie wood') as a suitable surface for outdoor velodromes rather than the softer and more porous pine.

The Vel d'Hiv, favourite haunt
of Ernest Hemingway, hosting
a six-day race in 1947.

88 Keirin

Track racing has been popular since the 1890s, with the first World Championships taking place in 1893, followed by its inclusion in the first modern Olympics in 1896. The sport remained popular until the 1940s, after which it fell from favour, apart from in Japan, where there is a particular form of track racing that continues to draw around 57 million spectators a year to more than 70 specialist tracks around the country. That sport is keirin – or 'racing wheels' – the popularity of which has not flagged since the first race took place in Kokura City in 1948.

The sport is something of a phoenix, rising from the ashes of World War II as a result of the Bicycle Racing Act of August 1948. This allowed cities to use profits from cycling events to rebuild shattered infrastructure and Kokura City – mooted as the drop site for the atomic bomb that eventually fell on Nagasaki – was quick to exploit the act. The first event, held on 20 November, 1948, raised over 19 million yen in betting receipts. Other cities followed suit and in 1957 the Japanese Keirin Association was formed to regulate the sport.

The traditional Japanese keirin is a mass-start race more like a dog or horse race than a traditional track event, with riders slowly circling the track to allow spectators to check them over before placing their bets. Blood type, astrological sign, thigh measurement and season-long form are just some of the considerations taken into account when punters place one of seven different types of combination bets involving the placement of two or three riders, so scrutiny is intense. In order to make it easier for spectators to follow, in 2002 the colours worn by the nine men who take to the track were standardised and are now white, black, red, blue, yellow, green, orange, pink and purple.

The first three laps unfold slowly behind a pacemaker, with each rider jockeying for position. Once the pacemaker pulls off the track and a bell is rung, it's every man for himself over the final two laps, with speeds frequently reaching in excess of 70kph. With a certain amount of barging and bumping tolerated and the vertiginous angle of the bank, crashes are not uncommon. Some riders consequently wear plastic body armour to avoid the worst injuries.

The sport is big business, with the best riders earning around 1.5 million euros (US$1.5 million) a season. As a consequence, Japanese keirin specialists rarely compete overseas even though the race has been part of the track World Championships since 1980 and the Olympics since 2000. In these events, the riders are paced by a small motorbike, known as a derny, although not in Japan. This may be done by another cyclist or occasionally a tandem.

Riders in the sport's home country must attend the specialist Japan Bicycle Racing School at Shuzenji, founded in 1968, to learn the skills they need to make it to the top. Only 150 riders make the grade after surviving a training regime best described as Spartan. Occasionally, foreign track riders attend – Australian Shane Perkins and Frenchman François Pervis among them. Although the average age of a rider is 35, it's not uncommon for racers to compete into their 50s, and the oldest-ever rider, Uemura San, was 60 when he finally retired.

Keirin is an overwhelmingly masculine world – women's keirin racing was suspended in Japan in 1969 through lack of interest from the paying public – but its inclusion as a women's Olympic track event in 2012 has sparked such renewed interest that in 2014, 15 Japanese women underwent the rigours of training at the Bicycle Racing School.

Keirin riders in action at the
Kokura Velodrome in 1954, in
Kokura, Fukuoka, Japan.

Modern timing methods permit riders to be split by hundredths of a second, meaning that there is now always a clear winner of a one-day event or a stage or the leader's jersey, even if it appears to the naked eye that the race is a dead heat.

One such close finish occurred during the team time-trial in the 2009 Tour de France, when spectators held their breath after Lance Armstrong's and Fabian Cancellara's teams appeared to cross the line with the same time. If the result stood, Armstrong would take the *maillot jaune*, an achievement that would signal his comeback from retirement. However, it was not to be: Cancellara was judged to be just 22 hundredths of a second faster than Armstrong in the overall standings and the Swiss rider kept the yellow jersey.

In previous decades, before the ability to measure time was so refined, this would simply not have happened. For instance, in 1929, on stage seven of the Tour de France between Les Sables d'Olonne and Bordeaux, three riders ended the day with seemingly the same time on a manual stopwatch and the next day's stage thus started with André Leducq, Victor Fontan and Nicolas Frantz all wearing a yellow jersey. Today, those riders would have been separated by hundredths of seconds and just one would have sported the coveted jersey.

Though the stopwatch had been used to determine the winners' times at the first modern Olympics in 1896, it wasn't until 1932 at the Los Angeles games that a finish line camera and chronometer – a stopwatch accurate to $1/10$ of a second – were used. The major leap in timing technology came in 1948 at the Winter Olympics in St Moritz, where a photoelectric cell – which was activated when the winner blocked the laser beam it was set up to receive – was used for the first time.

By 1952, automatic time stamping had been introduced that was accurate to within 100th of a second. Throughout the 1970s, timing technology was being continually refined with the introduction of computers and GPS, and for the 1992 Albertville Winter Olympics, electronic photo-finish technology was fully integrated into timing mechanisms. When Abraham Olano and Evgeni Berzin dead-heated on stage seven of the 1996 Tour de France it was the last time it could or would happen in the race, since transponders were introduced at the Olympics later that year for cycling and the marathon. The final piece of the puzzle was in place and the timing process was now fully automated.

Transponder or chip timing works on a radio frequency identification (RFID) system. Each rider's bike is fitted with a chip that transmits its unique code to radio receivers around the course, allowing a rider's time to be recorded and time stamped with great precision. GPS systems are also used in a team's race car to accurately calculate the time needed to catch a breakaway.

Despite this, the days of the stopwatch are not over. With new-found interest in the hour record, starting with Jens Voigt's record-setting ride in 2014 and currently held by Britain's Sir Bradley Wiggins, the presence of a coach at the trackside waving a stopwatch excitedly as a rider charges past has been revived. As if in homage, Voigt's disc wheels were finished to look like the face of a stopwatch.

Nicolas Frantz, Victor Fontan and André
Leducq were all awarded the yellow jersey after
stage 7 of the 1929 Tour de France, before the
advent of modern timing methods that can
pin-point a finish time to a fraction of a second.

Miscellaneous

90 Television

The first live television coverage of a sporting event was the 72 hours of transmissions from the 1936 Berlin Olympics, but it was to be another 12 years before the first live televised cycling race was aired – the final stage of the 1948 Tour de France, beamed in real time from the Parc des Princes. From those humble beginnings, however, the Tour has become the third-largest televised sporting event in the world, attracting the biggest audience after the FIFA World Cup and the Olympics.

Starting with a daily evening round-up, by 1958 live coverage from within the race itself – including the climb of the legendary Col d'Aubisque – was enthralling French audiences. In 1963, motorbikes carrying camera crew were allowed in the race for the first time in order to provide coverage of the final 30km of the day's stage. Ten years later, race organisers claimed a French audience of close to 20 million viewers.

Throughout the 1960s and 1970s, other countries started using similar motorbike and helicopter coverage to televise their own races and the programmes began to expand in terms of length and scope. By the 1980s, the Tour was being televised in the UK, USA and Japan, followed in the 2000s by Australia, China and Latin America. Nowadays, more than 120 broadcasters from around the globe beam their dedicated coverage to audiences of – if Tour de France race organisers ASO are to be believed – around 4 billion people during the three weeks of the event.

For cycling fans, bike racing and television are a perfect fit. Whereas hours spent on the roadside afford spectators only a brief glimpse of the riders, television allows those same fans access to events they might otherwise have missed. It does have its downside, however, and race coverage is a costly and difficult business, requiring a high level of expertise from the motorbike riders and helicopter cameramen who film the race. Screening it also plays havoc with television schedules when a stage overruns due to weather conditions and unforeseen race events.

It is all worth it for the viewing figures, though, a fact that prompted a boom in funding for the Tour: in 1960, when French national television broadcasters first paid for rights to televise the race, payments accounted for only 1.5 per cent of the total race budget. This has now risen to around 60 per cent – a huge percentage that has greatly benefitted the event and the sport in general.

This big money has, however, caused some teams to wonder whether the race should offer the kind of rights-sharing agreements that exist in other professional sports that have struck lucrative deals with broadcasters. This is unlikely to happen since it is enshrined in French law that the Tour de France must be screened on a free-to-air television channel, thus limiting the availability of digital television rights. This just goes to show the extent to which the Tour is venerated by the French, who consider free viewing of it to be their national right.

Fausto Coppi filmed by Cinesport in
1949. Live TV coverage opened up
the Tour de France to the world and it
is now viewed in over 120 different
countries worldwide.

91 Big green hands and corporate sponsorship

The last kilometre of a major race is usually packed with fans wearing branded cycling caps and brandishing oversized hands, providing the money shot for all the sponsors who help to make the race happen.

Perhaps most visible of all in recent years at the Tour de France has been an oversized green cardboard hand, advertising the green-jersey sponsors PMU. This is now one of the most prized pieces of promotional material handed out by the caravan – the extraordinary collection of vehicles that each year wend their way around the roads of France throwing out keyrings and pens, caps and sausages. In all, an estimated 14 million objects are handed out during the three weeks of the race from more than 150 vehicles. It takes around 45 minutes for the entire motorcade to pass by one spot along a route, which gives you an idea of the extent of the operation.

The fact that the introduction of the caravan in 1930 coincided with the race being contested by national teams for the first time was no fluke. In an effort to end the domination of the Belgian Alcyon team, Henri Desgrange decreed the Tour would henceforth be a competition between nations. This gave Desgrange something of a financial headache. How was he to cover the living costs of the cyclists who were now contracted directly to the race to ride for their country rather than riding for and being supported by trade teams, as was the case for all Tours of 1930–1961 and 1967–1968? The answer was the publicity caravan; by selling promotional places in the cavalcade of vehicles supporting the national teams, Desgrange was able to keep the race afloat.

This turned out to be a masterstroke. The caravan was an immediate success and has been a part of the Tour ever since, even though riders have competed in sponsored teams, not for nations, since 1969. Moreover, in addition to funding individual cyclists, advertisers also pay race organisers handsomely for their place in the procession, to the tune of some 150,000 euros to have three vehicles in the caravan according to some reports. This is money well spent for the sponsors, since the returns gained as a result of the exposure and increased brand awareness are extremely healthy – an estimated 5 euros per person who sees the brand's logo for every euro spent.

Not everyone has been so impressed by Desgrange's ingenious marketing coup, however. For instance, French playwright Pierre Bost wrote in 1935: 'This caravan of sixty gaudy lorries singing the virtues of an apéritif, underpants or a dustbin is a shameful spectacle. It stinks of vulgarity and money.' But for others the caravan brought razzmatazz, excitement and even the chance of a new career, as happened during the 1950s when the procession made a star of a young accordion player from Tarbes, Yvette Horner, who would stand atop a Citroen van playing her heart out. As Jacques Goddet, who had taken over responsibility for organising the event from Desgrange, wrote on the 50th anniversary of the race: 'It's a fete in the absolute sense of the term. That is to say, it's an occasion for people to get out of their routine, to forget their doubts, and take themselves to the place where a spectacle comes to you.'

Little wonder, then, that crowds flock to watch as they speed through the French countryside, and it is no surprise that the companies that bankroll the event capitalise on their presence by handing out branded freebies that people keep as mementos of the occasion, including the big green hands. These are no longer sponsored by PMU, and instead bear the logo of the Škoda car company, but remain just as collectible.

Yvette Horner, the young French accordionist who became synonymous with the Tour de France publicity caravan, playing at the 1959 race.

Dossard 13 and cycling superstitions

Since the earliest days of cycle racing, riders have carried out certain rituals or carried tokens to ward off the bad luck and frequent crashes that are part and parcel of life as a professional cyclist. For instance, it's not uncommon to see a rider kiss a medallion around his or her neck or make the sign of the cross after completing a stage. Other superstitions and rituals that have been reported include never eating the inside of a baguette (the crust is fine); never shaving your legs the day before a race (any nicks or cuts will sap your energy); and always wearing your undershirt exactly as it comes out of the washing machine, even if it's inside out.

Jacques Anquetil, the first rider to win five Tours de France, was also a keen student of astronomy, though his interest in science didn't protect him against triskaidekaphobia, the fear of the number 13. Indeed, such was the severity of his phobia, or so the story goes, that upon being told by a medium that an attempt would be made on his life during the Tour on the 13th of that month, Anquetil refused to leave his room. Fortunately, it was a rest day in the race and he was eventually persuaded to attend a lavish party thrown that evening by Radio Andorra and managed to brave the outside world.

The widespread triskaidekaphobia of cyclists can't have been helped by the fact that cyclist Tom Simpson died on 13 July during the 13th stage of the 1967 Tour de France. Perhaps as a result, if a rider is unlucky enough to be assigned *dossard* (race number) 13 he will usually pin one of the numbers on his jersey upside down, sometimes overlapping it with his second race number to make 3113, in order to counter the supposed jinx.

However, unlucky 13 isn't the only superstition associated with bike racing. There's a widespread belief among Italian riders, for example, that spilling salt will result in bad luck. Myths surrounding salt have been with us for thousands of years, dating back to the ancient Sumerians, Assyrians and Egyptians, who tried to counter the hex they believed spilling salt would bring by throwing a pinch over their shoulder, so the superstition is ingrained in many cultures.

Belief in this supposed jinx has transferred to the peloton, as shown by American cyclist Tyler Hamilton's telling of the story of an Italian teammate who deliberately dumped the contents of a salt shaker on the tablecloth. The next day, the Italian suffered a terrible crash, and thereafter Hamilton took to wearing a phial of salt around his neck, just in case. As he points out in his book *The Secret Race*: 'since there's so much we can't control, we do our best to make our own luck.' The day Hamilton forgot his talisman, he crashed and broke his leg, though whether this was due to him focusing on his forgetfulness rather than the road ahead cannot be determined.

Cyclists have a whole range of
superstitions, including around the
dossard 13. Here Sebastian Lang, riding
for Germany, wears the number 13 in the
traditional upside-down fashion.

93 White paint

Marking names or phrases on the road is a part of cycling tradition, though its origins are lost in the mists of bike-racing history. One thing is clear, however: cycling has always enflamed strong passions and engendered fierce rivalries that have often been commemorated by the white paint under the peloton's wheels. For fans, leaving their mark on the road in support of a favourite rider is more than simply a show of support – it's a way of saying 'I was there' months or even years after the event.

Cycling fans have always had strong allegiances for certain riders and teams, with sharp divides opening up, often along political or geographical fault lines. For the Italian *tifosi* (the superfans of cycling) in the 1950s, Fausto Coppi represented the modern, liberal face of the country while his great rival Gino Bartali stood for more traditional, Catholic values. In France in the 1960s, support was split between the northern bourgeois, who favoured playboy Jacques Anquetil, and the southern peasants, whose pin-up boy was Raymond Poulidor.

As cycling evolved and internationalised, so did the rivalries. Famous ones include the implacable Belgian Eddy Merckx versus the volatile Spaniard Luis Ocaña in the 1970s and, more recently, Belgium's Tom Boonen versus the Swiss Fabian Cancellara. Supporters of either side have latched on to this, and show their support by chalking or painting the names of their heroes on roads across Europe and beyond.

In the modern era rivalries have become team-based rather than being between individual riders. There is now intense competition between Belgian teams Lotto and Quick-Step, who played out their own grudge match during the one-day classics of the 2000s, and Team Sky and Tinkoff-Saxo, who have ignited the route of the Tour de France in recent years with their friendly rivalry. In response to this, and in order to get the public behind them, bigger teams now provide fan zones where spectators can follow their team through social media and TV coverage while waiting for the race to pass.

Not everyone approves of the daubing of messages of support (or, other less innocent messages and images) for cyclists on public roads and walls. When Yorkshire hosted the Grand Départ of the Tour, road painting including messages such as *'Allez Cav'* and *'Va Va Froome'* were removed from the A61 after the race, the local council citing complaints about 'graffiti'. Across the pond, the Tour of California has encouraged fans to use chalk rather than paint in recent years, saying they have received objections from residents about the practice.

White paint isn't the only potential source of aggravation for the organisers, and indeed it is relatively benign by comparison with the antics of the mankini-wearers and the streakers – who pose a very real hazard for cyclists as they jump into the road, as well as being distracting at moments when the riders need to concentrate. Perhaps the craziest of these show-off spectators, Didi Senft – known simply as 'the Devil' – is a German bicycle designer who has been attending the Grand Tours since the early 1990s. Clad in his trademark red costume and horns and brandishing a trident – the symbol he paints on the roads – Didi can be seen leaping and roaring encouragement as the riders race by.

Most fans, though, are simply content to watch and cheer without grabbing the limelight, their messages on the roads – whether in white paint or chalk – intended as gestures of support and goodwill.

Fans of Raymond Poulidor marking an umbrella with their favourite rider's name in white paint at the 1966 Tour de France.

94 Metal barriers

The earliest cycling races occurred on the open road, without security of any kind, leaving spectators and potential saboteurs free to impinge upon the course at any moment.

The first attempt to control overenthusiastic crowds at an event was made in the 1860s by a keen balloonist called Nadar when his balloon, Géant – featuring a two-storey gondola – was such a hit with the public on his visit to Brussels that he was forced to improvise crowd-control barriers using wooden trestles in order to keep spectators clear of the launch site. The idea took off, and wooden barriers were widely used at events until the 1980s. To this day, the Belgians refer to crowd-control barriers as 'Nadar barriers'.

The number of people standing on the roadsides of cycling races increased hugely with the introduction of paid annual holidays in the 1930s and by the time the metal barrier was invented in the 1950s, cycling was entering a golden age with Coppi, Bartali, Bobet and Kübler all vying to take home the biggest prizes in the sport. When the Tour de France resumed after World War II it was more popular than ever and there was a real carnival atmosphere by the roadsides. However, an incident at the 1950 Tour may explain why race organisers began to feel some measure of crowd control was necessary along the most popular stretches of the route.

In 1950, there was already bad blood between French crowds and the Italian riders as a result of an incident the year before, when a popular French rider had crashed and the Italian team had been blamed. Tensions were thus running high and on one of the early mountain stages, Gino Bartali – leading the Italian squad – was assailed by an angry drunken mob and knocked off his bike. The next day, Bartali withdrew from the race and took the other Italian riders with him, claiming he had been threatened with a knife. Clearly, something would have to be done to help prevent such incidents happening in future, and the use of barriers at busy spots where the attacks were most likely, seemed the sensible solution.

Fortunately, help was at hand. In the early 1950s, the metal barrier now so familiar at major cycling races – bedecked with advertising materials and hung with banners – was first patented by the French company Samia. A simple interlocking system of hooks and eyes made them easy to erect and they could be used to quickly form a long, impermeable chain of fencing, an ideal solution to the problem of aggressive spectators.

In the mountains, though, where barriers don't line the route (the logistics of setting up security barriers on narrow mountain passes are simply too difficult), things can still get hairy. With passions running high, punches and unknown liquids are still hurled at riders and they may be spat at. Looking on the bright side, though, this does mean that up where the air is thin or on the country lanes of deepest France, you can still see cycling in the raw, your view uninterrupted by metal barriers.

Despite the protection they offer riders, barriers are not always seen to be a good thing, and there have been several incidents in major races where metal barriers – whose feet often protrude into the road – have caused riders to crash, the most famous being the spectacular tumble taken by Djamolidine Abdoujaparov on the Champs-Elysées in the 1990s. Following more crashes caused by these barriers in the 2016 Tour, the riders' association CPA has once more called on the UCI to require event organisers to use flat-footed barriers in the final kilometres of major races, as well as placing the barriers and the crowds further away from the road.

In one of the most spectacular crashes in Tour de France history, Djamolidine Abdoujaparov, the 'Tashkent Terror', crashes into the protective barrier less then 100m from the finish line during the 1991 Tour de France.

95 Bidon

Since the very earliest bike races, cyclists have needed a method of transporting drinking fluids. Cue the bidon (the French for drinking bottle), a name derived from an Old Norse word *bida* meaning a 'drinking vessel'.

Originally made of glass and carried in a cloth bag on the handlebars, bidons were banned from the Tour de France in 1910 by Henri Desgrange on safety grounds after French rider Jean-Pierre Camdessoucens injured himself badly on the broken glass of his shattered bidon following a crash. As a result, from 1910 until 1937, bidons were made of welded tin instead, each 500ml container sealed with a cork and carried in a metal cage on the handlebars. Advertising began to appear on these in 1935, with Sanka coffee being the first to exploit the commercial possibilities. Next came aluminium cans, still sealed with a cork but now with a straw inserted in the centre – all the better for sipping the alcohol that many riders chose to consume between 1900 and the 1960s!

By the 1950s, bidons were being carried in bottle cages on the bike's down tube and sported the names of mineral water manufacturers, with first Vittel, then Evian, then Contrex sponsoring the containers used in the Tour de France. However, the biggest and most enduring change came in 1954 when the bottles started to be manufactured in plastic and sported a self-sealing cap – a design that has remained virtually unchanged to this day.

But what was in the bidon? This is where its history gets darker, and the innocent bottle is drawn into numerous stories involving skulduggery, cheating and the most intense rivalry in the sport's long history.

In the very first Tour in 1903, Hippolyte Aucouturier claimed to have been poisoned with a mixture of lemonade and sulphuric acid. In 1911, Paul Duboc was found vomiting horribly by the roadside on the descent of the Col d'Aubisque, the victim of a disgruntled ex-professional rider with a grudge and a known capacity for manufacturing suspect beverages.

Bidons have been abused in other ways too. In the 1953 Tour de France, the tiny French climber Jean Robic used a bidon made of lead to assist him on the descents, collecting these at the summits of mountains and discarding them at the bottom. Weighing only 60kg (132lb or 9st 6lb) in his cycling gear, his bidon added a full 9kg (20lb) to his weight and greatly increased his momentum.

Perhaps the most famous image of a bidon in cycling history is the one that shows a bottle being handed between two of the sport's greatest rivals, Fausto Coppi and Gino Bartali, during the 1952 Giro. This act is as surprising as it is iconic, given that their rivalry was so intense that both men had withdrawn from the 1949 World Championships rather than help the other to win. Yet on the slopes of the Col de I'Iseran, Coppi was photographed appearing to hand a bidon to Bartali. Or did he? Despite the goodwill depicted in the image, the picture re-ignited the enmity between the two Italian riders, with Coppi claiming that he had made the gesture and Bartali flatly denying it, saying: 'I did it. He never gave me anything.'

Today, it's almost impossible to estimate how many bidons a professional cycling team will get through during a race like the Tour de France, though the French newspaper *Nouvelle Observateur* puts the figure at 2376 drinking bottles per stage. These are passed to the riders either from the team car or are carried by riders in their musettes (*see* pp. 212–213) and contain water and sports recovery drinks. Bidons are not tested, and the responsibility for their contents rests with the teams.

The prize that every fan wants to take home,
the simple plastic bidon helps to keep a rider
properly hydrated through six hours in the
saddle. Jean Robic is shown collecting a
bidon at the 1953 Tour de France.

96 Musette

It may only be a simple cloth bag, but the musette is a welcome sight to a famished cyclist. Designed with a long strap to be easily passed from soigneur to rider – but only inside the official feed zone – once discarded they are a prize catch for the roadside fan.

The word musette comes from the Old French *muse* meaning 'bagpipe' and these small, highly portable bags were first used for cycling in the 1890s. Later, they were also employed to carry essential items by American troops in World War II, the most popular being the M-36 musette bag that was worn on the back like a rucksack. The standard-issue G519 military bicycle used during the same period was also often equipped with a (non-standard issue) musette bag.

The style of the traditional musette – a simple square or rectangular bag with a long strap for hanging round the neck – has remained unchanged since they were first used for bike racing; its design is the very definition of 'if it aint broke, don't fix it.' Despite its effectiveness, though, not all riders always use them. For instance, in the 1960s the Italian rider Gianni Motta was famously pictured eating a bowlful of pasta in the middle of the peloton.

Even if the bag itself hasn't changed, its contents have, and the food the musettes contain represents a history of the changing nutritional trends in the sport. In the early days at the turn of the 20th century, riders ate anything they fancied (often carb-heavy foods that would sustain them), but by the 1950s, a rider might find small sweet tarts and bananas in his musette. Skip forwards 30 years to the 1980s and the food had changed again, as is evident from soigneur Shelley Verses' recollections of filling her rider's bags with chocolate bars and mini sandwiches wrapped in pictures torn out of *Playboy*. Today's cyclist can expect to find slightly less thrilling but perhaps more sustaining gels, energy bars and rice cakes alongside bidons filled with water and a sports drink.

The feed zone – or *zone de ravitaillement* – is a popular spot for fans watching a race. Discarded musettes are highly collectable and team-branded examples sometimes sell on online auction sites for high prices, although it is likely that the opportunities for fans to nab one of these will now be limited. This is because the UCI ruled in 2015 that in any UCI-sanctioned race there must be a waste zone before and after the feed zone where riders must dispose of empty bidons, food wrappers and musettes – an attempt to prevent littering – although the fine for failing to comply is only 50 Swiss francs.

The simplicity and ease of use of these handy little bags is not confined to the professional peloton. Its small size but large capacity makes the musette the ideal bag when you're pounding out the miles. Once emptied, it can be easily stored in a jersey pocket or pannier for the ultimate in portability. Little wonder, then, that musettes for recreational cyclists are everywhere, in fabrics ranging from hardwearing canvas to Harris tweed and even the signature monogrammed leather of Louis Vuitton, and often sporting the names of cycling clubs or cafés or other brand logos.

Belgian rider Félicien Vervaecke collects his food bag or musette during the 1936 Tour de France. The musette developed from the military bag of the same name.

97 Ball bearings

As English cycling historian John Pinkerton once noted: 'Think of a new idea in bicycle design and someone will have already invented it, probably in the nineteenth century' – a statement that certainly holds true for the genesis and development of the humble ball bearing.

When J.K. Starley pulled together a series of technological innovations into the coherent design of his safety bicycle, he was quick to credit Joseph Henry Hughes – who had patented an improved ball bearing for bicycle wheels in 1877 – writing that: 'he was due a large share of the credit for the perfect cycle that we have in use today.' In fact, although ball bearings had been patented more than 80 years earlier by Philip Vaughan for use in the carriage industry, they were never used for bicycle manufacture. It was a French bicycle mechanic, Jules Pierre Suriray, who had first patented a method for manufacturing bicycle ball bearings in 1869, and these were used on the high-wheeler on which James Moore coasted to victory in the first-ever bicycle road race.

Whichever version you deem the more notable, however, there is little doubt that ball bearings played an important role in the development of the bicycle. This is because with the pedals connected directly to the front axle, it was important that the axle could rotate smoothly and freely – too tight and pedalling would be laborious, too loose and pedalling would be ineffective. Ball bearings mounted in two circular cups and fitted around both ends of the axle proved an effective solution. Add the fact that ball bearings are a vital addition to the wheel hubs, the bottom bracket and the fork tube and you can understand how important they are.

The science is simple – the spherical shape of the ball bearing allows two surfaces to roll over each other, thus greatly reducing the friction that might otherwise slow them down. Suriray's hand-ground ball bearings had one drawback, however: they deformed quickly under pressure. The race was thus on to manufacture the smoothest, most durable and friction-free ball bearings.

One of the leaders was German entrepreneur Friedrich Fischer, who had been experimenting with ball bearings since 1875 and developed his own grinding machine in 1883. By 1887, he was mass producing millions of perfectly true metal spheres at his factory in Schweinfurt. In 1896, the factory was producing 5 million ball bearings a week. Meanwhile, back in England, Joseph Henry Hughes had in 1877 patented single-row ball bearings – a single row of balls in a threaded, coned case that could easily be adjusted for wear – a system that was until recently the basis of most cycle bearings. Today, sealed or cartridge bearings, which can be removed and replaced as a single unit, are more common.

As with other bicycle components, the development of the ball bearing also had huge implications for the fledgling automotive industry. This is perhaps most evident in the evolution of the Volvo, which owes its existence to Swedish manufacturers SKF, a company that developed self-aligning ball bearings in 1907. Eight years later, a subsidiary company called 'Volvo' was formed, and they developed their first eponymous cars in 1927. As if to drive home the connection, the name Volvo means 'I roll'.

Ball bearings were first used in the manufacture of the bicycle James Moore rode to win the first ever long-distance bicycle race Bordeaux–Paris, in 1869. Here, attendees at the first all-girls and women bike mechanics course at the Community Bicycle Center in Biddeford, USA replace ball bearings in the rear hub assembly of their bikes.

98 Lead weights

The basic geometry of the racing bicycle has changed little since the 1900s, but advances in frame-building materials mean that today's road bikes weigh less than your average Jack Russell terrier.

In 1996, the UCI surveyed the cycling scene and came to a decision. The sport, they decreed, should be about the athlete, not the bicycle he rode. The viability of carbon fibre as a bike-building material had produced a series of frame-building innovations – such as the Lotus monocoque that Chris Boardman rode to Olympic glory in 1992 – and bicycles simply no longer looked like they had previously. Horrified by what they saw as a technological arms race that was moving the sport away from its roots, the UCI put together the Lugano Charter (ratified in 2000) that aimed to stop technological innovation in its tracks and return the sport to its roots.

No longer would expensive, one-off prototypes be eligible in competition – all bicycles and their components would, at least theoretically, be available to any bike purchaser. It also set strict parameters for bicycle frames and components. For instance, a rider's saddle position was to be within 2.5 degrees of horizontal and a bicycle must weigh no less than 6.8kg (15lb).

There were sound principles behind the UCI's new rules. Ultra-lightweight bikes could prove difficult to control and there were arguments about structural integrity. Perhaps more importantly, it meant that developing cycling nations could at least stand a chance of competing on equal terms. For clarity, there was an accompanying list of UCI-approved frames and wheels. Despite this, however, even when abiding by the rules it was still possible to produce a perfectly legal bike that came in under the UCI's weight limit.

To understand why weight is so important, consider this: on a 5km climb, averaging around 7 per cent gradient, every extra 450g (1lb) of weight will cost a rider six seconds. In the marginal gains era that can make a significant advantage. So how could a team exploit the most cutting-edge technology and still stay on the right side of the rules? The answer was simple: add a few lead weights (or an extra chain inserted into the bike frame).

In practice, most teams have used the restrictions on minimum weight to innovate in other areas. Power meters add weight and functionality. Alloy stems and handlebars bend rather than shatter in the event of a crash. Electronic gear shifters employ a battery pack rather than cables – the weight gain that this produces being compensated for by its ease of use. Similarly, any weight penalty inherent in the use of disc brakes is offset by their superior performance.

The UCI have said they will review the weight-limit rule if manufacturers can prove that their bicycles are safe, retain structural integrity and handle well, and they may even scrap the weight rule altogether.

A member of Italian Saeco team puts weights on Gilberto Simoni's bike before the seventh stage of the 2003 Tour de France to meet the weight limit for bikes of 6.8kg set by the UCI.

99 Shoulder sling

When Britain's Chris Boardman retired from cycling, he told a reporter: 'I had to give up cycling at the age of 32 because I had the bones of an old woman.' So just why are extremely fit athletes, capable of riding for hundreds of kilometres at a stretch, prey to such brittle bones? A contributing factor is that the collarbone is inherently vulnerable during a bike crash – so fractures are common. However, cycling itself, as a non-weight-bearing exercise, is the main culprit.

Writing in *l'Equipe* in 2003, French rider Laurent Jalabert described the life of a professional cyclist: 'At heart a rider likes to ride and sleep. And above all no walking. The blood doesn't circulate properly, your legs quickly get heavy.' In his book *The Secret Race*, American Tyler Hamilton wrote about how out of shape he felt when not riding, and how he couldn't even take a short walk to the shops. Moreover, Hamilton was prone to injury, breaking his collarbone in 2002 and then again in 2003.

One of the causes of the high incidence of these injuries is the bone itself. The clavicle is the last bone to form in the human embryo and the last bone to harden in the human skeleton, and can snap like the weakest link in the chain when a rider puts out his arm to save himself after a jarring crash, as Fausto Coppi, Sean Kelly, Greg LeMond, Jean Robic, Lance Armstrong and many others discovered during their careers. Not that this necessarily stops the riders in their tracks: in the 1956 Giro d'Italia, Fiorenzo Magni rode for half the race with a broken collarbone. Biting down hard on an inner tube tied to his handlebars, as much to fight the pain as to steer his bike, Magni finished second.

In 1994, German researchers ran a study comparing the bone-mineral density (BMD) of weightlifters, boxers and cyclists. The cyclists, many of them elite riders, exhibited considerably lower BMD than their fellow athletes. Studies conducted in the 2000s on cyclists competing in the Masters category (riders aged 35-plus) showed that their BMD was far lower than that of men of their age who were non-cyclists. A 2008 comparison of long-distance runners and cyclists discovered that 63 per cent of the bike riders had osteopenia (below-normal bone density that can lead to osteoporosis) of the spine or hip.

Riders involved in more explosive, or higher-impact, forms of cycling such as mountain biking or sprinting have shown significantly better levels of BMD than their road-cycling colleagues. The low impact of putting in the miles is one contributing factor to this, but another may be the loss of calcium during prolonged exercise as the muscles repeatedly contract. Sweat is another consideration – a Tour de France rider will produce 135 litres of sweat over the three-week race. Minerals lost through sweating include calcium, of which a rider will lose several hundred milligrams during a single stage.

So what's the answer for the road racers? Follow the example of those weightlifters and hit the gym. Though weight-based strength-training has been around since the days of the Ancient Greeks, it is relatively new to the world of cycling, where the weight gains attributed to increased muscle mass have historically been undesirable. However, by putting stress on the bones, training with weights increases bone density, while squats, lunges and step-ups especially build up BMD in the trouble spots of the hips and spine. Weight training has other benefits too, as Scotsman Sir Chris Hoy, multiple gold-medallist and world champion in the explosive sprint events, said: 'You are also working on core muscles to keep that posture right — there's no point having strong legs if you can't transmit it in a straight line.'

After breaking his collarbone at the beginning of the race, a heavily bandaged Tyler Hamilton still managed to ride to victory in the mountains in stage 16 of the 2003 Tour de France.

100 Pasta

It's a classic image – a professional cyclist sitting down to a huge bowl of spaghetti – but with the rise of sports nutrition in the 1980s, many of the old nutrition myths passed through generations are being busted.

Scientists and doctors have been interested in the effects of diet on performance since ancient times, when the food eaten by Greek athletes was considered as important as their physical training and was overseen by a specialist called an aliptae. Although not scientific in the modern sense of the word, the observations and conclusions drawn did result in some consensus over the years, with high-protein foods such as cheese, fish and meat – consumed in sometimes staggering quantities – deemed beneficial for strength and athletic excellence.

A more scientific approach was taken in the early 1900s when German physiologist Nathan Kuntz began pioneering work into the way the body metabolised carbohydrate and used stored fat during exercise. This in turn spurred on Scandinavian scientists, who expanded on Kuntz's work of the 1930s, using it as the basis of one of the first nutritional studies related to athletes in the 1950s. The conclusion from this research was that increased carbohydrate intake had a positive impact on performance – a seemingly healthier step up from the practices of the 1900s, when alcohol and strychnine had regularly been used as performance-enhancers.

But sports nutrition as a distinct discipline did not emerge until the 1980s. Interestingly, this coincided with the increased use of sports supplements, although sports nutrition has more in common with exercise physiology and a raft of other disciplines broadly encompassed by the term 'sports science'. The advent of this fledgling science dramatically altered the way athletes trained and it became apparent that endurance athletes – who had once focused solely on their carbohydrate intake – might benefit from paying more attention to protein (so perhaps those Greek aliptea had been correct).

With the arrival on the scene of specialised training camps and power meters that measure power-to-weight ratios – the lighter a rider is the better he climbs – the optimum role that nutrition plays in performance has been realised. Gone are the days when soigneurs would advise riders to eat only the crusts of a baguette, replaced instead by a tailored and very specific diet backed by proven scientific rationale.

Modern cyclists typically consume between 5000 and 8000 calories daily when riding a three-week stage race. After a breakfast of porridge or an omelette and a fruit smoothie, they will then snack through the day on a variety of foods including nuts, rice cakes, energy gels and sandwiches. Once they climb out of the saddle the first priority will be to grab a protein drink to aid recovery and encourage rehydration. They may also have some rice for a quick carbohydrate boost – it packs more complex carbohydrates than pasta. Dinner may contain an adequate, not excessive amount of carbohydrate and some quality protein. Then a protein shake before bed to maintain muscle fibre and aid recovery. But whether a rider chooses rice, pasta or even quinoa after a ride, carbohydrate is essential to replenish glycogen stores and boost the fuel available to the muscles.

In order to ensure the nutritional needs of their riders are met, teams often travel with their own chefs and, in some cases, their own kitchen trucks. The psychological impact of eating a proper meal after a day in the saddle existing on energy gels and sports drinks is incalculable, and proper nutrition is now accepted as another piece of the marginal gains puzzle.

Vittorio Adorni, Jacques Anquetil and
Felice Gimondi enjoying a bowl of spaghetti
during the 1966 Giro d'Italia. However, rice
has now become the carbohydrate of choice
for the modern peloton.

Index